AVRO SHACKLETON

The mysterious world of maritime reconnaissance and anti-submarine warfare rarely receives much attention, and yet it has been a vital part of British military aviation since the earliest days of its existence. As a maritime nation, Britain's seas are the country's most impregnable - or the most vulnerable - borders. Through the dark years of the Cold War it was the Shackleton's crews that defended Britain's seas, flying long and tortuous missions over thousands of miles of ocean in an aeroplane design that originated in 1936. It was a cold, noisy, uncomfortable machine, designed with only functionality in mind. But its crews grew to love it, and the Shackleton's infamous "growl" became a familiar noise to generations of RAF air and ground crews around the world, and a noise that was greatly mis_____
the_____
airc_____
Lanc____ ramily, and the end of the RAF's long association with piston engines.

Tim McLelland
Series Editor
tim.mclelland@keypublishing.com

CONTENTS

Page 4
Chapter One
LANCASTER LINEAGE
The RAF looks for a new maritime reconnaissance aircraft and Avro creates the final derivative of its legendary Lancaster design.

Page 22
Chapter Two
INTO SERVICE
The first Shackletons are delivered to RAF Coastal Command while work progresses on a new variant of the aircraft

Page 40
Chapter Three
THIRD TIME LUCKY
While the early versions of the Shackleton settle into RAF service, a new derivative is conceived and manufactured

Page 58
THE AVRO SHACKLETON IN DETAIL

Page 82
Chapter Five
RETIREMENT AND RESURRECTION
The RAF's maritime reconnaissance fleet approaches retirement. But the Shackleton returns, ready for a new life in a very different role.

Page 98
Chapter Six
AIRBORNE IN THE SHACKLETON
John Botwood describes a typical Shackleton training sortie from RAF Ballykelly, during the 1950s.

For more than a century of aviation history and for further titles in this series, visit *www.aeroplanemonthly.com*

Aeroplane Icons: **AVRO SHACKLETON**
Editor Tim McLelland. **Design and Layout** Paul Silk.
Publisher and Managing Director Adrian Cox. **Executive Chairman** Richard Cox. **Commercial Director** Ann Saundry.
Distribution Seymour Distribution Ltd +44 (0)20 7429 4000. **Printing** Warners (Midlands) PLC, The Maltings, Manor Lane, Bourne, Lincs PE10 9PH.
ISBN 978-1-910415-22-1

Published by Key Publishing Ltd, PO Box 100, Stamford, Lincs PE19 1XQ.
Tel: +44 (0) 1780 755131. Fax: +44 (0) 1780 757261. Website: *www.keypublishing.com*

LANCASTER LINEAGE

The RAF looks for a new maritime reconnaissance aircraft and Avro creates the final derivative of it's legendary Lancaster design.

The Shackleton was a direct development of the Avro Lincoln, the mainstay of RAF's Bomber Command during the early post-WWII era. Originally referred to as the "Maritime Lincoln", the Shackleton was designed to incorporate a much wider fuselage, suitable for anti-submarine warfare duties and maritime reconnaissance. The Shackleton did retain the Lincoln's distinctive wing design and structure. *(Photo: Aeroplane)*

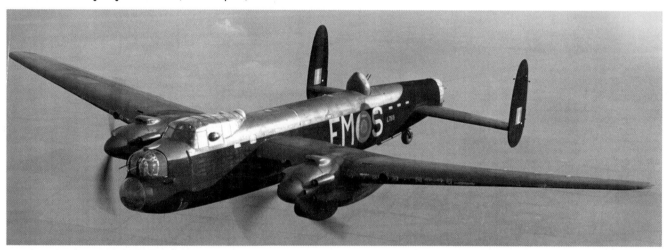

Created as a "Maritime Lincoln", the Shackleton retained the Lincoln's wing design and structure. The Lincoln wing was an extended derivative of the wing design that had been used for both the Lancaster and the Manchester (illustrated here) that preceded it. The Shackleton was therefore built on a design that had its origins in 1936. *(Photo: Aeroplane)*

It wasn't until the summer of 1991 that the Royal Air Force retired the last of its Shackleton aircraft, some forty years after the aircraft had first entered service. Although four decades of operational activity is not a particularly unusual achievement in itself, it is certainly remarkable that the aircraft withdrawn in 1991 was directly related to a design that was first conceived in 1936. The story begins in May of that year when the Air Ministry issued Specification P.13/36 for a new twin-engine "medium bomber" that would eventually replace the Whitley, Hampden and Wellington. In response to this requirement (or in anticipation of this, as it is believed that work on the design began some time before the Specification was actually issued) Avro's design team created a large but conventional

◄ Royal Aircraft Establishment Shackleton T.Mk.4 VP293, pictured landing at Farnborough during 1973. This aircraft was manufactured as an MR.Mk.1 variant, joining 236 Operational Conversion Unit in September 1951. It was converted to T.Mk.4 trainer standard during 1956. *(Photo: RAE)*

design, based on an extremely strong and durable centre section comprising a cantilever fuselage and bomb bay beam structure, which supported a huge wing centre section. The result was the Avro Manchester, an aircraft that demonstrated great potential but hampered by the engine that was chosen to power it. Rolls-Royce's Vulture "X-Block" engine was an ingenious development of an earlier design, with two Peregrine cylinder blocks mounted together to produce 1,760hp, but the engine proved to be woefully unreliable and it was de-rated to less than 1,500hp. Although the Manchester entered Royal Air Force service in 1940 the hopelessly unreliable Vulture engine effectively doomed the hapless Manchester to a premature retirement and the aircraft was withdrawn from bomber operations in 1942. However, Avro's unfortunate experience prompted Chief designer Roy Chadwick to look at ways in which the Manchester design could be improved by using Rolls-Royce's new

Merlin engine that was less powerful but far more reliable. Minimal changes to the Manchester airframe enabled four Merlins to be installed and the new Avro 693 (the Manchester III) duly emerged as the immortal Lancaster.

Given the outstanding success of the Lancaster, it was inevitable that Avro would look at further developments of the same basic airframe. When the Air Ministry issued Specification B.14/43 for an "improved Lancaster" suited to operations in the Far East (with greater range), Avro returned to the concept of extending the Lancaster's outer wings in the same way that the Manchester's wings had been modified to accommodate the Merlin engine. The Type 694 Lincoln looked very different to its Lancaster predecessor with a greater wingspan and longer fuselage, but the strong central fuselage structure and inner wing remained unchanged from the basic design that had been drawn-up in 1936. The Lincoln was a

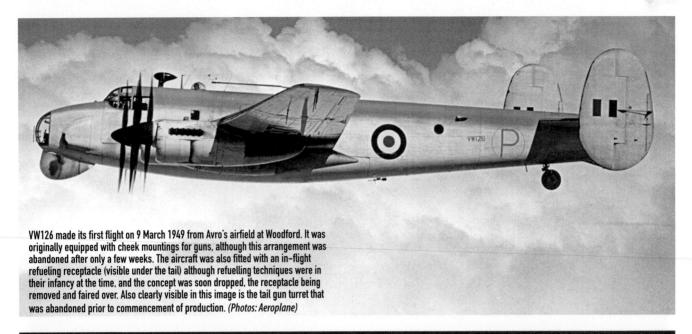

VW126 made its first flight on 9 March 1949 from Avro's airfield at Woodford. It was originally equipped with cheek mountings for guns, although this arrangement was abandoned after only a few weeks. The aircraft was also fitted with an in-flight refueling receptacle (visible under the tail) although refuelling techniques were in their infancy at the time, and the concept was soon dropped, the receptacle being removed and faired over. Also clearly visible in this image is the tail gun turret that was abandoned prior to commencement of production. *(Photos: Aeroplane)*

successful design but by the time that it entered service in 1945 the Second World War was over and the need for a Far East bomber immediately disappeared. Although effectively redundant, the Lincoln served with Bomber Command until the new Canberra jet bomber came into service, but Avro's design still had more potential to exploit, and the shifting requirements of the postwar era led to the Air Ministry's decision to develop the Lincoln into an aircraft capable of meeting the Royal Air Force's expanding maritime requirements.

During World War Two the RAF had employed a variety of aircraft types on Search and Rescue, Maritime Reconnaissance, and Anti-Submarine Warfare duties. Whilst most of these aircraft had been adequate for wartime use, they were often less-than ideal for the roles in which they were employed, and a large proportion had been supplied on a wartime loan basis, leaving the RAF short of

suitable aircraft in the immediate postwar era. In essence, the RAF needed two new aircraft types; one acting as a land-based replacement for the American Liberator, and the other being a replacement for the Sunderland flying boat. Although the war had ended, the RAF still had commitments around the globe and while a conventional land-based aeroplane would be suitable for operations within the United Kingdom and Europe, the RAF's operations in the Middle East and Far East were often better suited to the flexibility of the flying boat. But Britain's postwar economy required drastic cuts in defence spending and Britain's gradual withdrawal from many of its former Empire outposts led to a great deal of uncertainty over the RAF's future maritime requirements. The flying boat requirement quickly became an anachronism as Britain gradually withdrew from the Far East, and eventually the requirement was abandoned. The more

immediate requirement for a land-based reconnaissance aircraft was pursued with some vigour from the outset, largely because there was a growing recognition that the RAF's future maritime commitments would mostly be confined to the United Kingdom's coastal regions and the North Atlantic. It eventually became clear to both the RAF and political staff that only one aircraft type was really required to fulfill the RAF's tasks. Because of the pressing need to restrict defence spending, the design and manufacture of a completely new aircraft was not considered to be a serious option. This forced the Air Ministry to look at the modification of an existing aircraft, and Avro's Lincoln was the obvious choice. When Operational Requirement 200 was issued on 22 September 1945 it stipulated that the Lincoln should be adapted for long and medium range reconnaissance duties, this becoming Specification R.5/46 (eventually

◄ Pictured on 10 September, the second prototype Shackleton VW131 is seen at low level over Farnborough's famous Black Sheds with both starboard engines shut down. Also visible is a remarkable amount of skin buckling on the bomb bay door – skin peeling and buckling caused problems and delays during the earliest days of the Shackleton programme. *(Photo: Aeroplane)*

As development of the Shackleton continued, the RAF's Coastal Command retained its fleet of elderly Lancasters, modified for maritime reconnaissance and anti-submarine warfare duties. They were far from ideal for maritime operations and were becoming increasingly obsolescent during the early 1950s. The last example was withdrawn on 15 October 1956 when RF325 left RAF St.Mawgan's School of Maritime Reconnaissance for storage and eventual disposal at Wroughton. *(Photo: Aeroplane)*

After flight testing and trials work associated with the MR.Mk.2 programme, the prototype Shackleton VW126 was eventually transferred to the Royal Radar Establishment for use as a test bed for guided weapons research. Repainted in a Dark Sea Grey finish, the aircraft acquired an unusual chin radar housing and tail fairings associated with developmental work whilst based at Defford. After moving to Pershore, the aircraft was finally retired to No.2 Radio School at Yatesbury where it was dismantled in 1965. *(Photo: Robin. A. Walker)*

issued in March 1946). Adapting the Lincoln for land-based maritime reconnaissance might have seemed like a relatively simple proposal for the Air Ministry, but the Operational Requirement also specified that the new aircraft should be capable of carrying an extensive amount of specialized electronic equipment and that it should also provide the crew with an acceptable amount of comfort, given the considerable amount of time that they would be expected to spend inside the aircraft. It soon became clear to Avro that the existing Lincoln airframe wouldn't be capable of meeting the Air Ministry's requirements and that a new fuselage structure should be designed, which could be married to the Lincoln's wings.

This proposal was a logical step, especially when Avro had done something similar with the Lancaster, creating a completely new fuselage for passenger and cargo carrying, resulting in the York transport. The Lincoln's

wings and tail structure could remain unchanged, but the fuselage would be widened to provide a generous amount of internal space for both equipment and the ten-man crew. By January 1946 Avro had already produced the Type 696 design with a completely new (wider) fuselage, Lincoln-type tail and wings, and inner engine nacelles and landing gear adopted from the Tudor airliner project (Avro's civilian derivative of the Lincoln). The Air Ministry was greatly impressed by the proposed layout, with space for all of the necessary internal equipment, the crew stations, rest bunks and a galley, combined with sound proofing and heating.

► The Shackleton's fuselage structure, seen in cross-section during manufacture at Chadderton. Although the aircraft retained the Lincoln's wing layout, the Lincoln's fuselage (essentially the same as the Lancaster and Manchester) was too narrow to accommodate the equipment and crew required for maritime operations and it was therefore widened quite significantly. *(Photo: Aeroplane)*

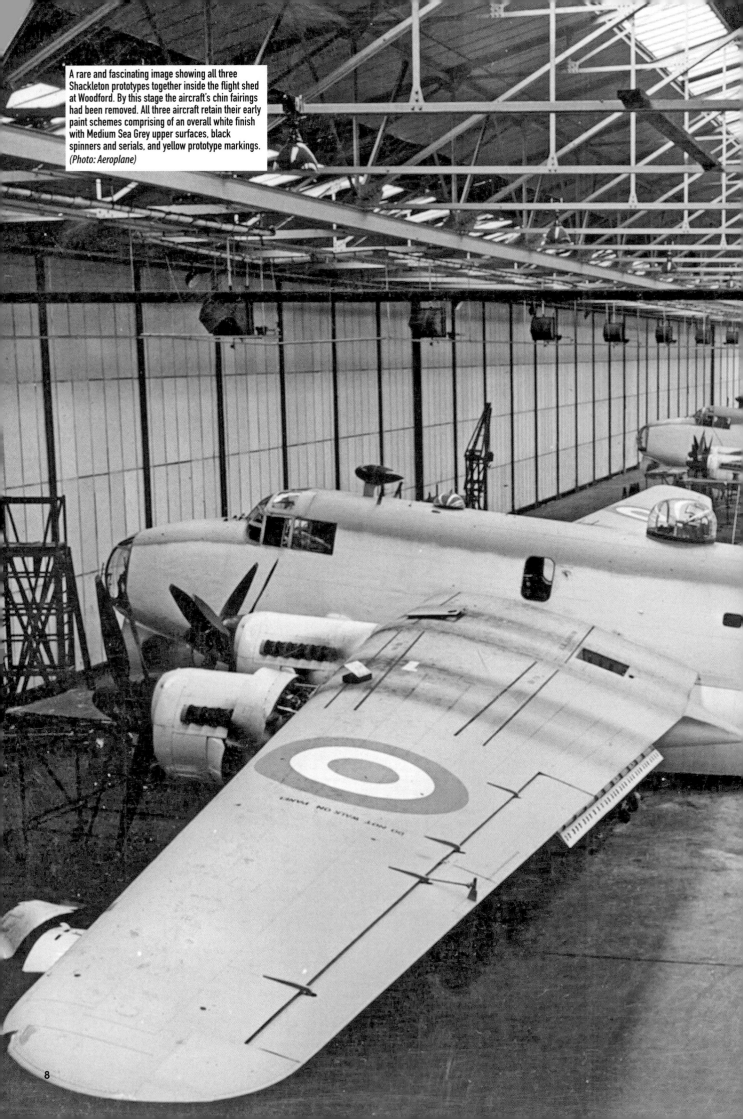

A rare and fascinating image showing all three Shackleton prototypes together inside the flight shed at Woodford. By this stage the aircraft's chin fairings had been removed. All three aircraft retain their early paint schemes comprising of an overall white finish with Medium Sea Grey upper surfaces, black spinners and serials, and yellow prototype markings. (Photo: Aeroplane)

The second Shackleton to emerge from Woodford was VW131, flying for the first time on 2 September 1949. As illustrated, the aircraft made an appearance at the 1949 SBAC Farnborough show just four days later, after having been put through a hurried ten-hour "shake-down" in order to qualify for appearance at the show. *(Photo: Aeroplane)*

VW131 performing for spectators in 1949, wings flexing as the aircraft begins a climb. After some years as a test vehicle, VW131 was transferred to Napier at Luton for a trial installation of Nomad E145 engines. The possibility of producing a new Shackleton variant equipped with these engines was considered for some time and VW131 was ultimately fitted with two such power plants but not flown at the time of the project's cancellation in 1955. The aircraft was dismantled at Luton in 1956, the fuselage moving to Bracebridge Heath where it was used by Avro for ditching research. *(Photo: Aeroplane)*

Nobody acknowledged the presence of two huge wing spars that cut straight through the fuselage for the crew to clamber over, perhaps because it was a slightly awkward illustration of how the core of the aircraft's structure had been designed way back in 1936. But Avro saw no reason to change the basic design, especially when the mighty Lancaster had demonstrated just how good it was. Although the Maritime Lincoln (as it was initially known) was primarily intended to be a reconnaissance platform, it was acknowledged that the aircraft might well be required to perform a limited offensive role, and that it would also need to be equipped with adequate self defence. It was not surprising therefore, that the design embraced the Lincoln's armament layout with both rear and upper gun turrets housing two

0.5in Browing guns and 20mm cannon respectively. The forward gun position was markedly different, thanks to the incorporation of a large glazed nose section that could accommodate an observer or a bomb aimer. With the gun turret position occupied, a forward-firing 20mm cannon was fixed in a "cheek" barbette either side of the new nose section. The Lincoln's capacious bomb bay provided more than enough space for almost any combination of bombs, torpedoes, or depth charges, and it is interesting to note that by February 1946 Avro had already drawn-up plans to enable the aircraft to carry a 12,000lb "sectional bomb" and the Vickers-manufactured Tallboy Type M. Provision was also made to enable the aircraft to carry a lifeboat (to be attached under the closed bomb bay doors).

Initially, Avro proposed the use of Merlin 85 engines and estimated the take-off weight as being around 82,000lb with a range of 2770nm, carrying a payload of 4,258lb at a speed of 200 knots. Range could be increased through the installation of a 400 gal auxiliary fuel tank in the bomb bay and a second tank could also be carried if the mid-upper turret was removed (this configuration only being necessary for long-range ferrying). Avro estimated that the aircraft would require a take-off run of around 3,440ft or 5,580ft to clear a fifty-foot boundary. The Air Ministry took a more pessimistic view, and although the precise nature of the relationship between Avro and the Air Ministry at this time is now largely unknown, it is clear that Avro struggled to meet the demands that were placed on the Maritime Lincoln as it was

Magnificent colour image of the third Shackleton, VW135. Flying for the first time on 29 March 1950 enjoyed a very short life as a trials aircraft, and in April 1954 it was dismantled for spares recovery by No.49 Maintenance Unit, at Colerne. *(Photo: Aeroplane)*

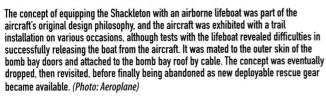

The concept of equipping the Shackleton with an airborne lifeboat was part of the aircraft's original design philosophy, and the aircraft was exhibited with a trail installation on various occasions, although tests with the lifeboat revealed difficulties in successfully releasing the boat from the aircraft. It was mated to the outer skin of the bomb bay doors and attached to the bomb bay roof by cable. The concept was eventually dropped, then revisited, before finally being abandoned as new deployable rescue gear became available. *(Photo: Aeroplane)*

The Shackleton's nose section was designed to accommodate an observer, situated on a forward-looking chair, with huge clear panels affording an excellent view ahead and below the aircraft. The design was simple (almost agricultural) but effective, although positioning the aircraft's search radar below the nose rendered the housing prone to bird strikes. After abandoning the cheek-mounted guns, there was no longer provision for any forward armament, and these factors were the primary reasons why the entire nose section was soon redesigned. *(Photo: Aeroplane)*

being created. One Avro memo stated that the Air Ministry should understand the "necessity for giving us final requirements" and that these should be "as close to Lincoln requirements as you can get" which suggests that Avro were either unable or unwilling to make any substantial changes or improvements to the existing Lincoln performance figures, even though the Air Ministry was clearly less-than-happy. But of course the Air Ministry was obliged to accept Avro's position, given that there was no other option on the table, and the Maritime Lincoln's projected range and payload figures were therefore changed to reflect the capabilities of the Lincoln, rather than the Air Ministry's aspirations.

Unusually, a contract for production aircraft was issued before any prototypes were ordered. Contract No.6/ACFT/6062/CB6(a) was placed on 21 March 1946, covering a batch of thirty Lincoln III aircraft, but it wasn't until 28 May 1947 that Contract No.6/ACFT/1077/CB6(a) was issued to cover three prototypes, these being VW126, VW131 and VW135. By this stage the Ministry of Supply had opted for Rolls-Royce's Griffon as the aircraft's means of propulsion, but only after a great deal of uncertainty had surrounded the issue of engine power. During 1946 Chadwick informed the Ministry of Supply that the existing design simply wouldn't meet the Air Ministry's requirements at the specified weight of 82,000lb. Chadwick claimed that the single-stage, single-speed Griffons were too heavy and that the Bristol Hercules would be a better option, enabling the aircraft to attain a range of 3,000nm if a

lower cruising speed and smaller offensive load was adopted. Chadwick claimed that if Griffons were used, the aircraft's weight would increase to 87,000lb and this would render all of Avro's stress and performance figures invalid, thereby causing a huge delay to the aircraft's development and delivery schedule. Other issues also arose including Chadwick's request that landing velocity stipulations should be relaxed and diving speed reduced to 300kts, as opposed to 340knts applied to the Lincoln bomber. Rather weakly, Chadwick insisted that the maritime Lincoln was a reconnaissance aircraft that would never be required to fly "corkscrew" evasive manoeuvres. The Ministry of Supply grudgingly accepted the various compromises, but remained unconvinced that Hercules engines should be used, chiefly

VP256 was the third production Shackleton MR.Mk.1. After making its first flight on 18 September 1950 it was transferred to RAF Manby for use by the RAF Handling Squadron, for preparation of the aircraft's "Pilot's Notes" publication. It then joined 224 Squadron and subsequently moved to Ballykelly, where it eventually joined 269 Squadron. On 26 October 1954 the aircraft was written-off when its pilot attempted to take-off with elevator locks engaged.

VW131 pictured in gloomy conditions at Woodford during 1950. A few weeks later the aircraft was in much brighter skies over Khartoum, where tropical performance trials were conducted. Arriving in October 1950, its return to Woodford was delayed until 18 November, following a bird strike. Three months later the aircraft was laid-up again after a pylon fell onto the aircraft at Boscombe Down, causing damage to the starboard wing and tailplane. *(Photo: Tim McLelland collection)*

▲ VP254 was the first production Shackleton MR.Mk.1, making its first flight on 28 March 1950, just one day after the first flight of the third prototype (which had been delayed pending installation of equipment). VP254 spent some time with the RRE at defford on guided weapons trials and after further test flying the aircraft joined 205 Squadron at Changi during May 1958. The aircraft's stay was short, and on 9 December tit crashed in the South China Sea.
(Photo: Tim McLelland collection)

◄ VP253, pictured towards the end of its relatively short existence, by which stage the aircraft appears to have been fitted with grey-painted Mk.57A Griffon engines. Although most of the aircraft's test flying was associated with armament and navigation trials, the aircraft was also used for testing sonobuoy launchers and camera installations.
(Photo: Tim McLelland collection)

Shackleton MR.Mk.1 VP257 is pictured over Westminster during the 1953 Coronation flypast over Buckingham Palace. The aircraft was then assigned to 220 Squadron at St.Eval and remained with this unit until January 1958 when it was withdrawn from use. *(Photo: Tim McLelland collection)*

First flown on 8 March 1952, MR.Mk.1 WG508 was assigned to 240 Squadron at St.Eval before moving to Ballykelly. The aircraft then returned to St.Eval and joined 206 Squadron (as illustrated). After a brief return to 220 Squadron, it completed its service life with 206 Squadron in March 1958. After being transferred to No.23 Maintenance unit it was sold as scrap in May 1963. *(Photo: Tim McLelland collection)*

Shackleton MR.Mk.1 WB823 joined 220 Squadron at Kinloss after making its first flight on 28 August 1951 and spending some time being prepared for service use by No.38 MU. The squadron moved to St.Eval during November 1951, where the aircraft is pictured during 1952. It was transferred to 206 Squadron in November 1956 and then moved to Ballykelly to join 240 Squadron in February 1958. It was placed in storage late in 1958 and sold as scrap during May 1963. *Photo: Tim McLelland collection)*

because specialized fuel would probably be required if the necessary performance was to be attained. But within weeks Rolls-Royce had digested the Chadwick's criticisms of the Griffon engine and proposed a new single-stage, two-speed Griffon connected to contra-rotating propellers that would be capable of absorbing the engine's additional power without any increase in propeller diameter. This was finally adopted for the Maritime Lincoln and by the end of 1946 both Avro and the Ministries had accepted that the aircraft would probably achieve a range of 2,600nm with a weight of 86,000lb, carrying a 4,000lb load. Provision for a jettisonable bomb bay fuel tank would provide additional range if this was necessary, albeit at the

expense of speed, and it was agreed that in-flight refuelling equipment would also be fitted, even though the technology for such systems was still in its infancy.

Throughout the initial design process the general configuration of the aircraft changed very little, the wing, engine nacelle and undercarriage arrangement unaffected by the changes in projected performance. The only substantial change occurred to the aircraft's tail surfaces, where wind tunnel tests eventually prompted the design team to adopt a new tailplane with wider chord mounted higher on the fuselage, combined with much larger end-plate fin and rudder assemblies. Despite retaining the Lincoln's wings, the Maritime Lincoln was gradually

regarded as a very different aircraft when compared to the Lincoln bomber, and it was agreed that it should therefore be referred-to as a completely new type with its own name. Roy Chadwick (who had become Technical Director after Stuart Davies had assumed the role of Chief designer) suggested that in view of his wife's relationship to the family of Sir Ernest Shackleton, the aircraft should adopt Sir Ernest's surname, bearing in mind its clear connections with maritime exploration, and the undeniable fact that (as Chadwick stated) the name had "a good ring to it." The Air Ministry agreed and the Avro 696 became the Shackleton GR.Mk.1 in October 1946.

Tragedy struck on 24 August 1947 when Roy Chadwick was killed, following the loss of

Photographs of Shackletons undergoing construction are extremely rare. This image is one of only a few surviving pictures of MR.Mk.1 aircraft in final assembly at Woodford. Three aircraft are visible on the production line while four Lancsaters are visible in the distance, undergoing modifications. *(Photo: Aeroplane)*

WB830 illustrates the overall Dark Sea Grey paint scheme that replaced the white and grey colours applied to early Shackletons. WB830 completed its maiden flight on 26 September 1951. It was delivered to 38 MU and transferred to 236 Operational Conversion Pilot Unit at Kinloss. Apart from a short stay with Rolls-Royce at Hucknall in 1954, the aircraft remained with the OCU and the Maritime Operational Training Unit (MOTU) that succeeded it in 1956. The aircraft was withdrawn in April 1960 and after being stored with 23MU the aircraft was scrapped in May 1962. *(Photo: Tim McLelland collection)*

◄ Pictured in August 1956, WB818 was the first in the second batch of Shackleton MR.Mk.1 aircraft ordered in 1949. Delivered to St.Mawgan in September 1951, it was ferried to Gibraltar to join 269 Squadron and remained with that unit until November 1959 when it was transferred to 205 Squadron. After being damaged in a taxying accident at Gan it was withdrawn in June 1961 and flown to Seletar to be placed in storage and eventual scrapping. *(Photo: Tim McLelland collection)*

◄ After serving with 42 Squadron, WG525 was transferred to 220 Squadron with codes T-P. It was moved to Avro's Langar facility for modification work in May 1957 (as illustrated) and in September 1958 it joined 205 Squadron at Changi. It returned to the Uk for repairs following a propeller bolt failure, but remained with 205 squadron until December 1960 when it was ferried back to the UK and placed in storage with 23 MU before being scrapped in August 1964.
(Photo: Godfrey Mangion)

the Tudor II prototype. Several members of the Avro team lost their lives, but the Shackleton's development didn't suffer any major delays, largely because most of the Shackleton's design had been settled by this stage. Stuart Davies assumed additional duties and oversaw the transition from design into production. By the end of 1947 the first engineering drawings had been issued to Avro's Chadderton factory and construction got underway with relatively ease, thanks to the Shackleton's relationship to the Lincoln design. With so many similarities, many of the construction jigs could be used immediately while many others required only small modifications. The minimum-change concept finally paid off and sub-assemblies were gradually completed and transported to Woodford by road during 1948, where they

were used to create VW126, the prototype aircraft. This machine was largely complete by January 1949, enabling Avro to move the aircraft outside at Woodford for some publicity photographs. Progress was swift and after a re-negotiation of the initial production contract (to reflect the many changes to the aircraft that had been made), during which one aircraft (VP253) was cancelled, the first aircraft was prepared for pre-flight testing. By March the aircraft had undergone fuel system tests and extensive engine tests, and the prototype was almost ready for flight. Avro's Chief Test Pilot J.H. "Jimmy" Orrell made a number of taxying runs during the first days of March, culminating in high speed runs along Woodford's runway, and with no significant problems having arisen, it was decided to fly the aircraft on 9 March.

Weather conditions on 9 March were typical of the Manchester region, with gloomy cloud cover restricting visibility to three miles and sometimes almost as little as one mile. But with a healthy 15kt north-easterly wind blowing straight down the runway, Orrell opted to begin the short 2,000ft journey to the runway threshold with S.E. Esler as co-pilot and A. Blake as flight engineer. Oddly, despite having taxied the aircraft quite extensively, it was at this stage that Orrell decided that the effort required to move the aircraft's rudder pedals was too great, and he slowly returned the aircraft to the flight sheds parking area, where Avro engineers quickly resolved the problem by applying patches of card and tape to the rudder. Improvised design was nothing new to Avro, and a similar approach had been employed on many

◄ Pictured during 1957, MR.Mk.1 WB846 was delivered to 38 MU in December 1951 and joined 224 Squadron two months later. It was transferred to 120 squadron in August 1954 and finally to MOTU in October 1956. It was withdrawn from use in March 1958 and became a ground instructional airframe at Kinloss as 7561M. It was scrapped a few years later. *(Photo: Tim McLelland collection)*

◄ Flying for the first time on 9 January 1952, WB856 was assigned to the Anti Submarine Warfare Development Unit at St. Mawgan three months later. It was transferred to 224 Squadron in September 1953 coded B-V, and after modifications at St.Mawgan the aircraft then moved to 240 Squadron (as illustrated) in January 1955. Two years later the aircraft was modified for use in Operation Grapple and joined 204 Squadron in June 1958. Placed in storage with 23 MU in February 1960, it was scrapped in December of that year. *(Photo: Ashley Annis)*

◄ VP257 made its first flight on 28 August 1950, attending Farnborough's SBAC show a couple of weeks later. It was delivered to 220 Squadron and coded T–P. The aircraft suffered a landing gear collapse on start-up during November 1952, and following repairs it rejoined 220 squadron recoded T–K. It was withdrawn to storage with 23 MU in January 1958 and scrapped during February 1963. *(Photo: Tim McLelland collection)*

earlier aircraft including the Lancaster, and even applied to the mighty Vulcan that followed some years later. Suitably modified, VW126 returned to the runway where Orrell opened-up its four Griffons to full power and released the brakes. Just fourteen seconds later the Shackleton gently lifted into the air and began a 33-minute test flight around the local area, watched from Woodford by many Avro representatives. After landing, further improvised modifications were made to the rudder surfaces and later the same day Orrell took the aircraft back into the air for a second flight, this one lasting 45 minutes.

These initial flights were an encouraging achievement, but the Shackleton was still the subject of many misgivings. Avro's designers still believed that he Ministry of Supply and Air Ministry were expecting too much from what

was a minimum-change development of an existing aircraft. The Lincoln had already effectively reached the end of its development potential and it was perhaps unreasonable to expect Avro to deliver significant improvements in range, speed and payloads with a design that was in effect already ten years old. Conversely, many officials within the Air Ministry were becoming increasingly convinced that pursuing a design that relied on outdated aerodynamics would be a mistake – a feeling that was compounded by the distinctly dated tail wheel undercarriage arrangement that so graphically linked the aircraft to the past rather than the future. Concern was also directed at the aircraft's projected crew facilities, which were undoubtedly going to be far superior to those found in the wartime Liberator or Catalina, but

still hardly adequate for the new Cold War era. Avro's test pilot J.D. Baker went to Malta to fly on a series of sorties with Nos. 37 and 38 Squadrons. Both units were operating Lancasters that had been modified for the maritime role at the end of World War two. After sitting-in on sorties lasting up to twelve hours, Baker returned to Manchester and prepared a report in which he acknowledged the improvements that the Shackleton would offer, notably the significant increase in space, rest facilities and a galley. But he also noted that the Shackleton would still be unable to deliver acceptable heating or ventilation, and that airframe vibration and noise levels would be almost impossible to reduce by any significant amount. Problems were also encountered with the prototype during the early test programme. The troublesome

Flying for the first time on 14 August 1951, WB820 was delivered to 38 MU before being issued to 224 Squadron in September, coded B–F. It was transferred to 269 Squadron (as illustrated) in January 1952 and moved with that unit to Ballykelly. During August 1958 the aircraft was withdrawn for conversion to T.Mk.4 standard. After conversion at Bitteswell it was assigned to the MOTO at Kinloss, moving to St.Mawgan in July 1965 coded S. It was withdrawn from use in December 1966 and placed on the airfield dump. *(Photo: Tim McLelland collection)*

◄ WB832 is pictured minus its outer wings at Avro's Langar factory, awaiting conversion to T. Mk.4 standard in August 1956. Built as an MR.Mk.1, it was issued to 224 Squadron in January 1952, transferring to 206 Squadron in October. After conversion it was assigned to MOTO in April 1958 still coded G. After Phase II modification it was returned to MOTU coded U. Withdrawn in July 1965 it was ferried to 2SoTT at Cosford and used as a ground instructional airframe (7885M) but withdrawn and scrapped some years later. *(Photo: Tim McLelland collection)*

rudder surfaces required further design and modification work and the aircraft's centre of gravity was found to be too far aft. The aircraft's static vent system caused major disturbances to the flight instruments and a variety of repositioning trials had to be conducted before a satisfactory arrangement was found. Even more annoying was a troublesome airframe vibration that couldn't be solved, and the mid-upper turret was temporarily removed to address the problem until time could be found to re-investigate the problem at a later stage. On 20 April 1949 the aircraft flew to Boscombe Down to fly a series of calibrated take-offs at 80,000lb weight. Returning to Woodford the next day, the aircraft continued to make these short visits to Boscombe Down to take advantage of the establishment's superior facilities. Meanhile, work was progressing on the second and third aircraft, the latter (VW135) being used to develop the various changes to the aircraft's interior layout that were progressively required. The pilot's seating had to be redesigned and repositioned and various changes were made to the crew stations inside the fuselage, while Avro's designers examined the issue of propeller vibration, solved by a decision to tilt the engines downwards by two degrees on production aircraft. The discovery that the aircraft's centre of gravity was too far aft presented Avro with another problem, but the Air Ministry had made it clear that some members of the Air Staff didn't see any need to equip the

Shackleton with defensive armament. Avro therefore proposed that the nose and tail gun turrets should be removed together with the very heavy armour plating that was placed around the aircraft's oil tanks. This would create a weight saving of at least 2,800lb and improve the centre of gravity problem. It was also suggested that adding wing tip fuel tanks would give the aircraft an additional 330gal of available fuel. The Air Staff's reaction was indecisive, but the concept of reducing unnecessary equipment and "cleaning up" the airframe became the basis of what would eventually emerge as the Shackleton Mk.2. There was good news for Avro too, and with the first production contract (now revised to 29 aircraft) in place, an instruction to proceed with second contract for 38 aircraft was given on 18 May 1949.

It was eventually agreed that the aircraft's armour plating should be deleted and that the front and rear gun positions should be removed. Boscombe Down confirmed that the tail turret would seriously affect the aircraft's centre of gravity, and also concluded that the forward-firing nose guns (which could not move left or right) were virtually useless. An interim navigational systems layout was agreed (although it was accepted that this would need to be changed quite swiftly) and a number of other changes that had been proposed by the Air Ministry were abandoned or deferred in order to expedite progress. But at the same time the MoS also introduced new requirements, including the provision of a

bomb bay carrier system that would enable the Shackleton to act as a transport aircraft, supplementing RAF Transport Command's aircraft if required. Additionally, rocket projectile launch rails were requested, each unit capable of carrying eight 25lb or 60lb weapons. Avro's problems were then compounded by the news that the proposed lifeboat for the Shackleton might weight as much as 4,000lb and this would require the bomb bay to be strengthened in order to carry it. As if all of these difficulties were not enough, attention was slowly shifting towards the creation of what would become the Mk.2 Shackleton, and the MoS urged Avro to introduce this variant as soon as possible. The Mk.2 would eliminate the heavy fore and aft gun turrets, introduce a new, streamlined nose profile, a similarly streamlined tail fairing, and a completely new radar scanner position that would be placed under the rear fuselage. The GR.Mk.1 was equipped with ASV Mk.XIII radar that was housed in a cupola placed under the aircraft's nose, and although this was the ideal position for the radar, it was a less-than ideal position in terms of aerodynamic performance. The Mk.2 would eliminate this problem and create a much "cleaner" airframe that promised to deliver a range of around 3,000nm. Not surprisingly, the Air Ministry requested that Shackleton production should be switched to Mk.2 standard as swiftly as possible, and the Shackleton Mk.1 therefore became regarded as an "interim" aircraft long before it had entered RAF service. ❖

◀ ▲ Photographed during 1952, just a few weeks after delivery to 42 Squadron, WG529 is seen amongst the long grass at St.Eval. At this stage it had yet to receive its codes A–H, although the aircraft's glossy white and grey finish has already been sullied by streaks of soot and oil emerging from its Griffon engines. WG529 is also pictured some months later overseas, after having received its codes and a squadron badge applied to the nose glazing. The aircraft flew with 206 squadron until December 1957 when it was transferred to 240 squadron at ballykelly. It remained there until being withdrawn in August 1958, and was sold as scrap in 1963. *(Photos: Aeroplane)*

◀ ▲ These two images of WB837 with the Maritime Operational Training Unit illustrate the Dark Sea Grey paint scheme that was progressively applied to all Shackletons from the mid-1950s. It is first is pictured in 1961 after having been converted to T.Mk.4 standard, wearing an overall grey paint scheme combined with red serials outlined in white. The second image shows the same aircraft in 1965, when MOTU moved from Kinloss to St. Mawgan. By this stage all Shackletons were gradually receiving glossy white upper fuselages, designed to reflect heat from the aircraft's fuselage interior. MOTU also began to apply its own unit badge during this period, applied in black and white under the flight deck. *(Photos: Aeroplane)*

INTO SERVICE

The first Shackletons are delivered to RAF Coastal Command while work progresses on a new variant of the aircraft

WL796 pictured at Farnborough during September 1953. For the show, the aircraft carried a lifeboat under its bomb bay and (as can be seen) part of the flying demonstration was conducted with three engines shut down. The aircraft went on to serve with 38, 37, 204 and 205 Squadrons, finally being withdrawn in October 1967 before being scrapped the following year. *(Photo: Aeroplane)*

Shackleton MR.Mk.1 VP289 was photographed for "The Aeroplane" during 1958. These top-quality images show the Mk.1 Shackleton in remarkable detail, during a photographic rendezvous over Portrush and surrounding areas. The Shackleton's "patchwork" of riveted stringers and skinning is clearly evident, as is the huge amount of staining over the wing surfaces. This was reduced significantly when later Shackletons were upgraded to Phase II and Phase III standard and the Griffon engines were fitted with exhaust pipes. *(Photos: Aeroplane)*

Although test flying with the prototype was underway, RAF Coastal Command became increasingly concerned at the Shackleton's scheduled entry into RAF service. Largely equipped with elderly Lancasters that were far from ideal for the Maritime Reconnaissance role, Coastal Command was eager to get the Shackleton into service as swiftly as possible, but the continual changes to the aircraft's configuration (ironically, often as a result of requirements that were introduced by the Air Ministry) served to delay progress. The second Shackleton prototype (VW131) made its first flight on 2 September 1949, still equipped with the abandoned tail turret and nose-mounted guns, although the in-flight refuelling system had been removed. An intensive period of flying enabled the aircraft to attain the necessary ten hours of flying that qualified the aircraft to appear at the 1949 SBAC Farnborough show in September, and test pilot Johnny Baker put the aircraft through its paces on each day of the show, although the spectators were unaware that he was obliged

to sit on a pile of cushions with wooden blocks attached to the aircraft's rudder pedals, pending changes to the flight deck design. By the end of September the rocket projectile armament option was dropped and the requirement to carry a 12,000lb store was also abandoned. Test flying was temporarily suspended while the tail and nose armament was removed from both prototypes and VW131 received modified split rudder tabs before flying recommenced in January 1950. The third prototype (VW135) completed its maiden flight on 29 March, and although the aircraft was largely similar to the first and second prototypes, the third aircraft emerged with the tail and nose guns already removed, and with the navigator's window deleted. Meanwhile, VW126 completed manufacturer's trials and subsequently went to Hatfield where de Havilland investigated what had become a persistent vibration problem. It was thought that modifications to the rear propeller blades might provide a solution although the MoS proposed the abandonment of the contra-rotating

propellers in favour of conventional four-bladed assemblies. Cropping of the rear blades proved to be successful, and Avro's design team turned their attention to the aircraft's inadequate heating system and the persistent issue of noise suppression.

VW131 went to Boscombe Down during May 1950 for acceptance trials. Limited to 86,000lb and with a maximum speed of 262kts over 82,000lb, diving speed was restricted to 290kts because of tailplane strength problems, but the Boscombe Down pilots eventually reported that in overall terms the aircraft possessed good handling characteristics, despite being unacceptable for service use in its present condition. It was reported that the rudders were heavy, the ailerons were unresponsive and even though the aircraft's asymmetric qualities were good, the aircraft was tiring to fly in almost all conditions. Stalling was reported as acceptable with wings remaining level although there was little warning of an impending stall. In a turn the stall was far less acceptable, with severe wing drop occurring.

Glide approaches without power could be performed comfortably although rounding-out above the runway at a speed of 115kts required hard manoeuvring and ran the risk of propeller "discing" in which aerodynamic drag was created, rendering the elevators ineffective. Avro immediately embarked on a series of programmes to fix these deficiencies, and all three prototypes became heavily engaged in trials that ranged from tropical testing (based at Khartoum) to external stores clearances. Just one day after the third prototype made its first flight the first production Shackleton GR.Mk.1 (VP254) also took to the air, although the aircraft was an unequipped airframe that didn't begin flight testing for many weeks. The second production aircraft completed its first flight

on 30 June and Contract 6/Acft/5047/CB.6(a) was issued for a further 20 airframes. During September VP257 performed at the SBAC Farnborough show and VP256 went to RAF Manby's Handling Squadron for preparation of the RAF's Pilot's Notes. On 19 December the RAF revised its nomenclature and the Shackleton GR.Mk.1 became the MR.Mk.1, reflecting the aircraft's maritime role. The first eight Mk.1 Shackletons were assigned to testing, distributed between Woodford, Boscombe Down, the Telecommunications Flying Unit at Defford and the Central Servicing Establishment at Wittering. Initial CA release was given on 31 January 1951 although tropical operations were limited to 72,000lb because of continuing engine cooling problems (water methanol injection

was to be introduced to solve this problem). At long last, and despite many difficulties, the Shackleton was ready to enter RAF service.

VP258 was the first Shackleton MR.Mk.1 to be delivered to the RAF, flying to No.38 Maintenance Unit at Llandow on 7 March 1951 for installation of service equipment. Further aircraft soon followed although the first three were still fitted with unmodified elevators that had not been fitted with increased area ahead of the hinge line. VP260 became the first Shackleton to be delivered to an operational unit, arriving at Kinloss on 30 March where it joined No.120 Squadron. The first deliveries were all subject to various standards of modification, and while some aircraft still had unmodified elevators, all of the initial deliveries were configured for

Shackleton MR.Mk.1 VP289 low over Portrush during a sortie from home base at Ballykelly. *(Photo: Aeroplane)*

revised navigator positions and sonobuoy receiver station layouts, in anticipation of new equipment that had yet to be delivered. The inner and outer Griffon engines had different air filters, and these required two sets of spares to be held by RAF squadrons and Maintenance Units. In order to avoid this complication, the engine filters were revised for the second batch of aircraft (beginning with WB818, which first flew on 1 August) and the Shackleton's outer engine nacelles were slightly enlarged in order to accommodate the standardized engine. Later Mk.1 aircraft were equipped with Griffon 57A engines that were more reliable with provision for intermediate power settings, and these were progressively fitted to earlier aircraft as they became available. It was this modification

that led to the use of the term "Shackleton MR.Mk.1A" but there is no official recognition of this designation, therefore it seems likely that it was used only informally by some air and ground crews. By the beginning of 1952 the Shackleton was effectively cleared for operational use and on 26 February the first of the third batch of deliveries (WG507) made its first flight from Woodford, with the final MR.Mk.1 (WG529) being delivered to Llandow on 18 July. Replacement of Coastal Command's Lancasters was finally underway, although the Air Staff was still far from confident that the Shackleton was the most suitable aircraft for its requirements.

Although Coastal Command's squadrons were now receiving the first Shackletons, there was no plan in place to replace the

Lancasters operated by the School of Maritime Reconnaissance at St.Mawgan. The RAF had already determined that a modified version of the Varsity crew trainer would be most suitable for the School, but with no decision having been made, a bid for a fleet of 22 Shackletons was put forward. The Varsity had demonstrated some potential as a maritime reconnaissance platform, and with plans still being made to develop a new flying boat (chiefly for overseas commitments), the Varsity seemed to be ideal for short and medium range over UK waters. By the end of 1950 the Varsity was the primary candidate for the short-range maritime reconnaissance role, while the longer-range Shackleton would be more suitable for patrols far out over the Atlantic where German U-boats had

Shackleton prototype VW126 pictured during July 1951 after having been modified to represent the proposed Shackleton MR.Mk.2 configuration. The nose section was replaced by a completely new section, although the glazed observer's position was fashioned from metal, as the aircraft was only intended to investiage the aerodynamic properties of the new layout. The ventral radar scanner (empty) was also fitted and a reshaped tail section (with a clear rear portion) was also attached. The aircraft spent a considerable amount of time with the A&AEE at Boscombe Down, while the properties of the new variant were investigated. *(Photo: Tim McLelland collection)*

WB833 was the true prototype of the Shackleton MR.Mk.2. Taken from the MK.1 production line, it first flew on 17 June 1952 and subsequently went to Boscombe Down for evaluation. It spent time with Avro at Woodford and with the RAE before being transferred to RAF charge during November 1960 when the aircraft went to the Anti Submarine Warfare Development Unit at Ballykelly. It remained there until 1964 when it was upgraded to Phase III standard and assigned to 210 Squadron coded T. It remained with the Ballykelly Wing until 19 April 1968 when it crashed in bad weather conditions on the Mull of Kintyre. *(Photo: Aeroplane)*

operated with impunity during World War Two. In reality, the Shackleton was also barely capable of reaching such distances but the Varsity represented a more economical solution to at least some of the Coastal Command's requirements. It was estimated that with a nominal rate of 65 flying hours per month out to a range of 600nm, the Varsity would cost £15,539 compared to the Shackleton's cost of £18,930. But with cost considerations being of such importance, the prospect of obtaining Neptunes from the USA as part of the postwar Military Aid Programme was a far more attractive proposition and a bid was made for fifty of these aircraft. The Varsity option was no longer pursued, and the School of Maritime Reconnaissance eventually acquired Shackletons to replace their Lancasters, the final example (RF325 – the RAF's last operational Lancaster) being

retired in October 1956. The trainer version of the Shackleton Mk.1 was based on the conversion of existing airframes that swiftly became redundant as new-build Mk.2 Shackletons came off the production line. VP258 was used as a trials aircraft and ten aircraft were modified to T.Mk.4 standard at Avro's Langar facility. Externally the aircraft were unchanged apart from the removal of the mid-upper turret, but internally the layout was changed considerably with additional training equipment installed and a radar operator station replacing the rest bunk area. As with so many aspects of the Shackleton programme, difficultiues soon arose and Avro's fatigue testing revealed that the aircraft's safe life expired at 3,600 hours, at which stage the huge centre section structure required what was almost a complete rebuild. This meant that the "new" T.Mk.4 aircraft

would have only approximately 1,500 of available flying hours before they would require major rebuilds. Despite this, the Air Ministry opted to continue with T.Mk.4 conversions and during August 1957 the first two aircraft (WB837 and WG511) entered service with St.Mawgan's Maritime Operational Training Unit (successor to the SMR). Eventually, a further seven aircraft were ordered although the last of these was not converted until October 1960.

The various problems that surrounded the Shackleton Mk.1 encouraged both Avro and the Ministry of Supply to look towards a completely new version of the aircraft that incorporation a variety of very necessary modifications. This process began at a very early stage and the first draft of revised Specification R.5/46 was issued on 14 December 1949, before the first production

The first in a contract for 40 Shackleton MR.Mk.2 aircraft issued in December 1950, WL737 is pictured at St.Eval during 1953 whilst assigned to 220 Squadron. During August 1958 it moved a couple of miles south to St.Mawgan with 42 Squadron and by 1966 it had move to Ballykelly, joining 210 Squadron coded Z. It then moved to Singapore to join 205 Squadron coded J, returning to the UK for storage during October 1971. It was scrapped at St.Athan during 1973. *(Photo: Tim McLelland collection)*

Three views of WG531, one taken by Avro's photographer while the aircraft was assigned to manufacturer's trials at Woodford. After making its first flight on 21 August 1952, the aircraft appeared at that year's SBAC show, before returning to Woodford for cabin heating trials. It was then transferred to St.Eval (as illustrated) as part of the Station Flight, for evaluation of cabin conditioning and noise levels. In April 1954 it was transferred to 42 Squadron. It was officially declared as missing on 11 January 1955, having probably collided with WL743 south-west of Ireland. *(Photos: Tim McLelland collection)*

GR.Mk.1 had even flown. Most importantly, the aircraft's disappointing range performance had to be improved, and Avro anticipated that the aircraft's endurance could be increased significantly if the nose and tail profile was streamlined and additional fuel capacity was introduced. As part of this process Avro eventually determined that the radar housing would be relocated in a retractable "dustbin" that would extend from the underside of the rear fuselage. The Mk.1's fixed tail wheel would be replaced with a retractable twin wheel assembly, and with additional fuel capacity the modified aircraft would have a range of at least 2,600nm when carrying a 4,000lb weapons load. Further draft specifications were produced, although the various improvements that were outlined were a result of developments that were being achieved by Avro, rather than being

aspirations coming from the Air Ministry. Even the perennial issue of noise suppression was raised again, but too much emphasis on this matter was avoided, because it was accepted that any significant improvement would probably be unattainable. The possibility of fitting the aircraft with wing tip fuel tanks was eventually abandoned when stress calculations revealed that such modifications would have a serious affect of the wing's fatigue life, and as an alternative Avro looked at designing tanks that could be carried under the outer wing's attachment point, but this option was also eventually dismissed. The decision to redesign the aircraft's nose profile was soon complicated by the Air Staff's wish to reintroduce armament, but it was determined that the Boulton Paul Type L nose turret could be fitted within a more streamlined housing that would enable gun

or cannon fire to reach five degrees elevation, fifty degrees depression and twenty degrees in azimuth, with the bomb aimer's position moved to a glazed panel underneath the turret. Other less obvious changes were also made, including a revised braking system with toe brakes for differential steering and the introduction of control surface spring tabs. Thicker Perspex windows and engine tail pipes (instead of ejector exhausts) were expected to reduce noise levels, but not by very much. The aircraft's camera installation was also modified, and the low/medium level day/night camera equipment was shifted to pneumatically operated cupolas positioned under the tail. Contract 6/Acft/6129/CB.6(a) was issued in December 1950 for a batch of 40 Shackleton MR.Mk.2 aircraft, followed by 6/Acft/6408/CB.6(a) covering a further 40 aircraft in February 1951, whilst requesting that existing contracts should be modified to allow introduction of the Mk.2 aircraft into the Mk.1 production line as swiftly as possible.

The prototype Shackleton VW126 was temporarily withdrawn from test flying early in 1951 and Avro's engineer's embarked upon the process of removing the aircraft's forward nose section at its separation point directly underneath the flight deck windscreen. Simultaneously the rear fuselage was removed just ahead of the tail structure and the new proportions of the Mk.2 design were introduced. The rear fuselage was rebuilt to incorporate the new tail wheel assembly, rudder and elevator locking devices (for ground steering), while the redesigned nose profile was fashioned from plywood and metal, to act as an aerodynamic test specimen. The new radar housing was assembled in dummy form and fixed into the lower fuselage, and the aircraft's hydraulic and pneumatic systems

were modified to accommodate the radar, tail wheel and camera installation systems. In this revised form the aircraft made its first flight on 19 July 1951, once again in the hands of Jimmy Orrell. A great deal of development work was then conducted from Woodford until 14 May 1952 when VW126 was declared ready to go to Boscombe Down for handling tests. By this stage WB833 was almost complete, having been withdrawn from the Mk.1 production line and modified to Mk.2 standard as a production-standard prototype. It made its first flight on 17 June 1952 and although being fully representative of the MR.Mk.2, the nose turret was not yet ready for installation. Less than a week after its first flight WB833 also went to Boscombe Down, where further evaluation was conducted, although a great deal of equipment and systems were so similar to the Mk.1 aircraft that further evaluation was unnecessary. The ASV Mk.13 radar was judged to be

satisfactory and capable of detecting the conning tower of a submarine at a range of up to 8nm from a height of 500ft, while a fully surfaced submarine could be detected from 20nm. These results were not as good as those obtained by the AN/APS-20 radar fitted to the Lockheed Neptunes that were now beginning to arrive from the US, but the American radar did suffer from "clutter" that often made the radar picture difficult to interpret. Initial CA Release was issued on 17 December but once again a limitation on tropical operations was imposed, as engine oil cooling had still not been resolved. It wasn't until 1954 that a solution was found when WR964 was fitted with Griffon 57A engines, equipped with larger oil coolers, although trials conducted from Khartoum demonstrated that at temperatures of 45 degrees (Centigrade) the engines still overheated and the Ministry of Supply had to settle for a limit of 41 degrees if these coolers were to be retrofitted to existing

RAF St.Mawgan's South Pan during 1967, with Shackleton T.Mk.4 WB837 parked outside the station's huge servicing hangar. WB837 was originally delivered to 220 Squadron as a standard MR.Mk.1 aircraft, but it was converted to trainer configuration during 1956 at Langar. It joined MOTU at Kinloss during August 1961 coded H. Moving to St.Mawgan in 1965 coded W, it remained active here until May 1968 when it was delivered to 27 MU at Sahwbury and placed in storage before being scrapped in February 1969. (Photo: Urs Beittig collection)

airframes that were all eventually equipped with Griffon 57A engines. Further attempts were made to reduce engine noise and Rolls-Royce was instructed to manufacture properly-engineered tail pipes for the Griffon engine exhaust. These were fitted to VW126 early in 1953 and although they resulted in a reduction in noise of some seven decibels in the forward portion of the fuselage, the rear crew positions reported an incre4ase in noise output of some 3 three decibels. Further trials on production-standard aircraft revealed that virtually all of the noise reduction had been achieved through improvements in fuselage soundproofing and by July the modified engine exhausts had been abandoned.

Installation of Boulton Paul's Type N turret proved to be relatively trouble-free and the two 20mm Mk.5 Hispano cannon worked perfectly, even though some Air Ministry officials still wondered whether the

armament was needed. Rather more troublesome was a persistent vibration when the guns fired, and the cordite fumes that spread through the aircraft interior. Various fixes were tested including additional doors and extractor systems but the final solution was a simple one – opening the pilot's side windows. Further aft, aerodynamic breaker strips were fitted to the inner wing leading edge (and retrofitted to Mk.1 aircraft) to improve stall warning characteristics, and the previously-cancelled rocket projectile installation was reintroduced for use with the Glow-worm night illumination system. But after trials on WG532 and installation on a small number of aircraft, the system was once again abandoned. Rather more successful was the autolycus ion-mobility spectrometer designed to detect the exhaust gases from enemy submarines, and this was to be fitted in the aircraft's nose section, albeit at the expense of stowage space for eight

sonobuoys. WL791 was displayed at the 1953 Paris Air Show and WL796 was demonstrated at the 1953 SBAC Farnborough show, test pilot Johnny Baker performing a spirited display routine that even included a single engine flypast, despite the presence of a bulky Mk.3 lifeboat under the aircraft's bomb bay. Trials with this lifeboat proved to be another source of problems for Avro, and a great deal of time was devoted to the development of reliable release techniques, only to find that the Air Staff's requirement for the lifeboat was to be cancelled.

The first Shackleton MR.Mk.2 aircraft to enter operational service were WG555 and WG556, both arriving at St.Eval on 12 January 1953 (with WG554 following a couple of weeks later). By this stage Coastal Command's re-equipment with the Shackleton was well established. Following the delivery of Mk.1 Shackletons to No.120 Squadron and No.236 Operational

◀ ▲ MR.Mk.2 WR960 is pictured at Horsham St.Faith during 1956 and low over the sea off Lands End during a photographic rendezvous in 1958. Making its first flight on 5 February 1954, the aircraft joined 228 Squadron coded P (as illustrated). It then moved to 228 Squadron in August 1958 coded X (illustrated), before moving to 210 Squadron at Ballykelly during December 1960. After modification to Phase III standard the aircraft went to 205 Squadron in February 1968, before returning to the UK in November 1970. It was then modified to AEW. Mk.2 standard, entering service with 8 Squadron during June 1972. It remained in use as an AEW platform until 22 November 1982 when it was flown to Cosford, becoming 8772M. It was transported to the Greater Manchester Museum of Science and Technology in January 1983 and remains on display there on load from the RAF Museum. *(Photo: Aeroplane)*

MR.Mk.2 WG555 is pictured at St.Eval, basking in Cornish sunshine. Assigned to 42 Squadron, it was modified to Phase I standard and transferred to 210 Squadron coded U. Modification to Phase II standard saw the aircraft move to 204 Squadron coded N, and finally it was upgraded to Phase III standard, ev entualy returning to 204 Squadron coded K. It was assigned to the Majunga Detachment Squadron during March 1971, returning to Honington in February 1972. It's last flight was to Catterick on 9 May 1972, before being allocated to the RAF Fire Fighting School there. *(Photo: Tim McLelland collection)*

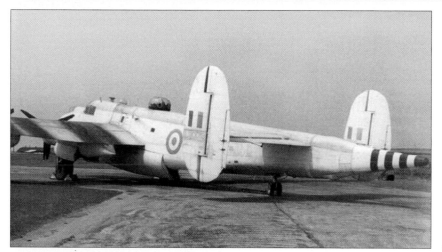

WL789 completed its maiden flight on 10 June 1963 before being ferried to No.38 Maintenance Unit at Llandow on 15 July. Whilst under the care of the MU it was modified by an Avro working party to carry a Magnetic Anomaly Detector (MAD) system, in anticipation of a fleet-wide modification programme. For this purpose the MAD sensor was housed in a long boom attached to the rear of the aircraft, painted black and white to prevent ground clearance damage. It was assigned to the Anti Submarine Warfare Development Unit at St.Mawgan in September 1953, coded F-D. Various modifications were made to the aircraft but the MAD system was found to be unworkable in the Shackleton, thanks to the aircraft's problematical magnetic signature and vibration problems. Eventually the aircraft was repainted grey with red serials (the MAD boom painted red and white), but the project was abandoned in 1958 and the aircraft was restored to MR. Mk.2 Phase II standard before joining 224 Squadron in April 1959. It subsequently served with 38 squadron and 205 squadron before being withdrawn in August 1967. *(Photos: Arthur Pearcey & Tim McLelland collection)*

Conversion Unit at Kinloss, it had been the turn of No.224 Squadron (based at Gibraltar) to relinquish its fleet of tired Halifax aircraft and take delivery of new Shackletons. No.220 Squadron was next to reform with Shackletons at Kinloss, before moving south to St.Eval during November 1951, after which No.269 Squadron received Shackletons over at Gibraltar, although this unit moved to Ballykelly in March 1952, while No.120 Squadron moved to Aldergrove. The next unit to equip with the Shackleton MR.Mk.1 was No.42 Squadron at St.Eval (June 1952) and finally No. 206 Squadron reformed in September, also based at St.Eval in Cornwall. The arrival of the first Mk.2 aircraft for No.42 Squadron in mid-January 1953 marked the beginning of a new era, although a Mk.2 Shackleton had in fact already been seen near St.Eval more

than a week previously when WG553 was delivered to the Anti Submarine Warfare Development Unit at nearby St.Mawgan. It was decided that each maritime squadron would receive three MR.Mk.2 aircraft while the number of MR.Mk.1 aircraft assigned to each unit would be reduced to five. Initial experience with the new Shackleton variant was good, although a considerable number of aircraft found themselves tucked away in hangars for long periods due to lack of spares. This frustrating situation eventually prompted one Commanding Officer to declare his squadron non-operational until the spares situation was eventually resolved. Another problem arose when US authorities refused an application for additional Neptunes to replace the Lancasters operated by No.37 based at Luqa. These elderly Lancasters were suffering from major

corrosion problems and it had been hoped that Neptunes could swiftly act as replacements, but when the proposal was refused it was necessary to deliver a fleet of eight new Shackleton MR.Mk.2s to the unit, the last of these arriving in January 1954, by which stage No.204 Squadron had also reformed on Shackleton Mk.2 aircraft (although two MR.Mk.1 aircraft were also nominally assigned to the unit) at Ballykelly. Back in Malta, No.38 squadron reformed on Shackleton MR.Mk.2s during September 1953. The process of gradually replacing the remaining MR.Mk.1 aircraft progressed over the following months until spring 1955 by which stage the RAF boasted nine UK squadrons and two overseas squadrons, all operating the Shackleton MR.Mk.2, leaving the GR.Mk.1 and T.Mk.4 in service only with second-line units.

Shackleton MR.Mk.1 was delivered to Gibraltar-based 224 Squadron in October 1951, coded B-H. It then transferred to 269 Squadron and moved to Ballykelly, before heading to Kinloss for a period of service with 236 OCU. It was then converted to T.Mk.4 standard at Langar with final modifications being carried-out at Waddington by a team from nearby Bracebridge Heath. It then went to MOTU in July 1957, coded V. After a short spell with the KInloss Station Flight, it returned to MOTU until withdrawal in June 1968 when it was ferried to Stanstead and assigned to the airport fire school. It was eventually destroyed on site and removed as scrap.
(Photo: Urs Beittig collection)

The Shackleton MR.Mk.2 proved itself to be a reliable machine that was liked by both air and ground crews, despite the inescapable fact that aircraft were often found to be unserviceable and spent a great deal of time laid-up in hangars while relatively minor "fixes" were undertaken. But in January 1957 the Royal Aircraft Establishment concluded that the aircraft had a safe fatigue life of only 3,600 flying hours, meaning that a major wing spar repair and modification programme would have to be put into place. The situation became rather more urgent during June 1958 when fatigue testing showed spar fatigue at a much earlier stage, resulting in the temporary grounding of all Shackletons that had flown more than 2,150 hours. An urgent repair programme was put into place and aircraft were rotated through Avro's

Langar facility where they were modified for a safe life of at least 5,000 hours. This process was completed remarkably quickly, with Varsity aircraft being temporarily assigned to maritime squadrons for training purposes until all Shackletons were back in service by November. Further modifications to the Shackleton MR.Mk.2 were planned as part of an ongoing programme of improvements that would be introduced as new equipment became available. The improvements would be introduced as packages referred-to as "Phases" and the first of these began in 1958 when was new ASV Mk.21 radar was cleared for service use, and other modifications were ready for introduction, including a "Blue Silk" Doppler system and a new station for a Tactical systems operator. The modifications were performed by Avro at Langar or by No.49

Maintenance Unit at Colerne after trials were completed on WL797. Phase II was already being planned before Phase I had been completed and WB833 went to Boscombe Down during October 1958 to begin testing new equipment. Trials took longer than expected and it wasn't until 1960 that Phase II updates were introduced into the MR.Mk.2 fleet. New equipment included new sonobuoys, a "Violet Picture" UHF homer system (replacing an earlier VHF set), new intercom, a UHF R/T system, a sonobuoy homer, a new radio compass, and an "Orange Harvest" electronic counter measures system. The long-abandoned engine exhaust pipes were finally fitted too, not because the Air Ministry had suddenly taken a more serious interest in noise suppression, but because the original ejector exhausts were often breaking off

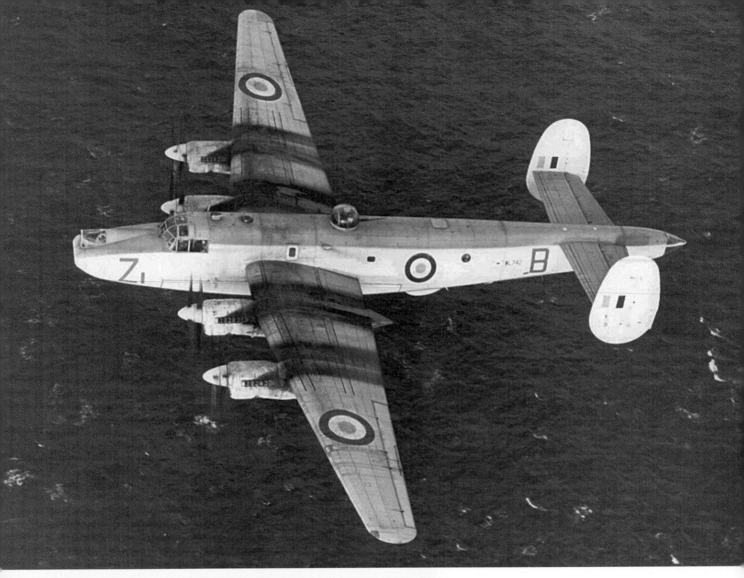

▲ WL742 graphically illustrates the huge streaks of black staining across its wing surfaces, caused by the filthy exhausts of its Griffon engines. Coded B-Z, the aircraft is pictured whilst assigned to 206 Squadron in 1953. The aircraft subsequently flew with Nos. 42, 224, 203 and 204 Squadrons before being retired in April 1967. *(Photo: Tim McLelland collection)*

◄ ▼ Shackleton MR.Mk.2 WG532 was retained by Avro, following its first flight on 12 September 1952. Operating from Woodford, it was fitted with rocket projectile launcher rails and used for carriage and release trials of the Mk.8 rocket projectile. It was subsequently transferred to the ASWDU in January 1953 for Glow Worm trials, and didn't enter regular squadron service until October 1954 when it joined 42 Squadron. The concept of equipping the Shackleton with rockets was soon dropped, and the system was not fitted to any other aircraft. After moving to 120 Squadron, the aircraft was modified to Phase I standard and issued to 224 Squadron coded S. Following modification to Phase II standard the aircraft went to 205 Squadron in August 1966 coded E and remained with this unit until being withdrawn in August 1967. The aircraft was scrapped at Shawbury during September 1968. *(Photos: Tim McLelland collection)*

WL751 from 224 Squadron was delivered in May 1953 coded B-L. It was subsequently repainted with a union flag on the tail surfaces replacing the usual national insignia, together with a new code "3" on the aircraft's nose, in preparation for the squadron's tour of South America in 1957. When the aircraft was eventually retired in May 1972 it was flown to Baginton and sold to a civilian company that subsequently sold the aircraft as scrap. The aircraft was recovered by Hawker Siddeley Aviation in anticipation of re-sale to the Confederate Air Force in the USa but the plan never materialized and without another buyer the aircraft was finally scrapped in January 1975. *(Photo: Tim McLelland collection)*

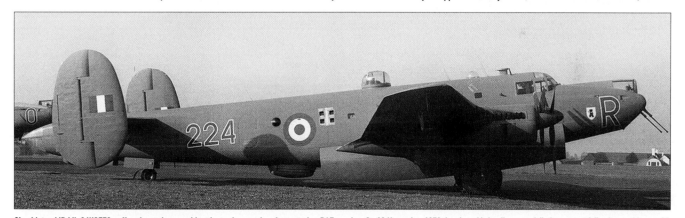

Shackleton MR.Mk.2 WG558 suffered a serious accident just a few weeks after entering RAF service. On 10 November 1953 the aircraft's landing gear failed to retract following problems with the tail wheel that had "cocked" at an angle. On landing the starboard main gear collapsed as the undercarriage selection switch was still in the "up" position. The aircraft was repaired by February 1954 and the aircraft joined 224 Squadron in an overall Dark Sea Grey paint scheme with red serials and other red markings outlined in white. *(Photo: Tim McLelland collection)*

and becoming jammed inside the engine cowling, causing a fire risk. Weapon improvements were also made and a smaller Autolycus Mk.3 system was installed, and by the beginning of 1963 the last aircraft modified to Phase II standard was completed at Langar. Although not part of the Phase I or Phase II programmes, the Shackleton Mk.2's mid-upper turret was also progressively removed, not only because it was found to be an unnecessary source of weight, but because the assembly had partially collapsed in some airframes, and by the end of 1956 almost all of the turrets had gone.

The final update programme for the Shackleton Mk.2 began in 1963 when Phase III trials were undertaken using WG556. This aircraft was joined by WR960 (also modified to Phase III standard) fitted with recording cameras for weapons release trials associated with the upgrade. In addition to equipment and armament upgrades, more fundamental modifications were made to the airframe so that the wing spars were strengthened and the wing surfaces were re-skinned. Inside the aircraft the Tactical station was completely revised, and fuel capacity was also increased, the No.2 tanks being replaced by larger versions that brought the aircraft's fuel capacity up to

3,350gal while a fuel dump jettison facility was installed to enable fuel to be released from Nos.2 and 3 tanks in the wing. A four-tube flare discharger was fitted and the main undercarriage units were modified to handle the increased all-up weight of the aircraft, which had risen to 96,000lb. Attention was finally given to crew comfort too, and a new heating system was introduced comprising four heating units that fed the flight deck, main cabin and bomb bay. New (thicker) soundproofing material was fitted in the fuselage and new sound-absorbing floor covering was installed, although problems with the

This impressive air-to-air photograph dated 15 October 1955 shows for Shackletons from No.228 Squadron on a formation training flight from their home base at St.Eval. Painted in glossy Medium Sea Grey with red serial numbers outlined in white, union flags are applied to the aircraft tail surfaces in preparation for Operation Suntan, a goodwill visit to South America. *(Photo: Aeroplane)*

Happy faces as the crew of WG510 from No.42 Squadron arrive at their aircraft, out on a windy dispersal at RAF St.Eval. All of the crew wear standard equipment for Shackleton operations, with RAF blue-grey flying overalls and orange life jackets. Although caps and berets are being worn for this publicity photo, normal crew attire was a cloth earpiece set, with crash helmets for the pilot and co-pilot.*(Photo: Aeroplane)*

The final production Shackleton MR.Mk.2 was WR969, pictured here whilst serving with 220 Squadron, visiting RAF Bovingdon during 1957. It was operated by a number of different squadrons and converted to T.Mk.2 standard in 1967. It then joined MOTO and remained with that unit until it was modified to Phase III standard and reverted to MR.Mk.2 standard before joining 205 Squadron in November 1970. It was withdrawn in September 1971, flying to St.Athan for storage and eventual scrapping by the end of 1974. *(Photo: Tim McLelland collection)*

aircraft's centre of gravity led to the subsequent removal of this new flooring in the rear fuselage. Even the infamous Elsan chemical toilet was finally afforded curtains and washing facilities. Far more significant were the improvements to the aircraft's armament options, not least the provision for nuclear depth charges and new torpedoes. The Griffon engines were improved to Mk.58 standard with strengthened gearboxes that could cope with the demands of the larger 12 kilowatt, 28 volt DC generators that were necessary for the aircraft's more sophisticated avionics and navigation equipment, and exhaust pipes were finally fitted. The modification programme got underway late in 1966 with remaining aircraft being upgraded during the following year.

Meanwhile, another programme was underway to produce new trainer aircraft for St.Mawgan's Maritime Operational Training Unit (MOTO). Their fleet of T.Mk.4 aircraft (modified Mk.1 machines) had provided the

unit with a useful and reliable trainer, but having been used so extensively, a replacement was required and agreement was reached to convert ten Shackleton MR. Mk.2s into crew trainers. Logically, the new variant should have become the Shackleton Mk.5, as the Mk.3 and Mk.4 designation had already been allocated but, rather confusingly, it was decided that the new trainer would become the Shackleton T.Mk.2. WL739 was withdrawn from service with No.204 Squadron during September 1966 and ferried to the Langer facility that was now part of Hawker Siddeley Aviation. With the upper turret already removed, the only external modification required was the removal of the 20mm cannon in the nose turret, but inside the aircraft the rest bunk and galley areas were removed so that a new radar station could be installed together with student consoles. By the end of 1967 the conversion process had been completed and tested, and WL739 flew to St.Mawgan on 3

January 1968 to join the MOTU. The remaining nine aircraft were duly converted and the last of these (WR967) departed from Langar on 5 September 1968. During this same period in time, Hawker Siddeley (into which Avro had been absorbed) made some attempts to offer the Shackleton Mk.2 as an export product, although very little overseas interest was forthcoming. The most serious interest came from India, where elderly Constellations were still employed in the maritime role. Hawker Siddeley first proposed a version of the Shackleton Mr.Mk.2 Phase II, but subsequently offered India a version of the Phase II aircraft, without the option for nuclear weapons or the RAF's ECM system. Production of new aircraft was not anticipated but as RAF airframes became redundant it was expected that these could be bought back from the RAF and refurbished for re-sale. But India's interest soon waned and the Shackleton Mk.2 was destined to fly only with the Royal Air Force. ❖

Shackleton MR.Mk.2 WL785 of No.37 Squadron was one of a small number of Shackletons that participated in the RAF's operations during the 1956 Suez Crisis, flying ASW and SAR missions over the Suez region. Based at Luqa, the aircraft was painted with campaign colours on the rear fuselage comprising yellow and black bands. As can be seen, they were not applied with any great degree of skill. Although some reference sources claim that similar markings were applied to the aircraft's wings, there's no evidence to support this. *(Photo: Tim McLelland collection)*

This delightful photograph shows three Shackleton T.Mk.4 aircraft from the Maritime Operational Training Unit in formation over Cornwall during a sortie from their home base at St. Mawgan. The familiar china clay pits surrounding St.Austell can be seen in the background – a welcome sight for countless Shackleton crews recovering to St.Mawgan in typical foul weather. *(Photo: Wg.Cdr. K.S Rowe)*

Engine start-up at St.Eval as a Shackleton MR.Mk.1 prepares to embark on a training mission over the Atlantic. Clearly visible in this picture is the pilot's side panel window that could be slid open either on the ground or in flight – a particularly useful facility for Shackleton crews operating in climates rather more tropical than Cornwall. *(Photo: Tim McLelland collection)*

THIRD TIME LUCKY

While the early versions of the Shackleton settle into RAF service, a new derivative is conceived and manufactured

Shackletons were deployed world wide as part of the RAF's many commitments. No.37 Squadron was deployed to Aden's Khormaksar airfield in July 1957, replacing a detachment of 42 Squadron aircraft tasked with policing and defence of the Aden Protectorate, flying reconnaissance, bombing and strafing missions against rebel forces. The busy scene at Aden is pictured here during what appears to be a public display, with some of the Shackleton's weaponry on show.
(Photo: Aeroplane)

Pictured at St.Mawgan during 1970, WG533 was operated as a T.Mk.2 trainer for two years before being restored to MR.Mk.2 standard. Freshly painted, the aircraft is seen prior to making a long ferry flight to join 205 Squadron in Singapore. It returned to the UK in January 1972 for disposal. *(Photo: Tim McLelland collection)*

Shackleton MR.Mk.2 WR963 is pictured during 1963 whilst assigned to No.38 Squadron. Unusually, the aircraft's national insignia has been removed from the tail surfaces and replaced by a union flag and Royal Air Force titling. This was probably in preparation for an overseas goodwill visit. The squadron codes and the aircraft's serial are applied in red with white outlines. The aircraft is now in the care of the Shackleton Preservation Trust at Coventry. *(Photo: Ashley Annis collection)*

The continual improvements to the Shackleton's capabilities led to a gradual but inexorable increase in aircraft weight, which served to exacerbate what was already a less-than ideal range capability. Avro's designers were acutely aware of the difficulty and by 1952 they had drawn-up plans to make major alterations to the Shackleton airframe that would provide the aircraft with at least a further four hours of patrol endurance. To do this, the aircraft would need to carry an extra 800 gallons of fuel and Avro proposed that this would be achieved by fitting wing tip fuel tanks, as had been proposed for the Shackleton Mk.2. The possibility of using tip tanks had been abandoned when it was established that the wing structure couldn't adequately support such an installation, therefore the new Mk.2A aircraft would feature stronger redesigned outer wings that had tip tanks attached as standard. Additionally, the wing joints and spar booms would be much stronger, and the wartime-style tail wheel undercarriage would be replaced by a completely new tricycle arrangement that had originally been developed for the Ashton aircraft. Although this particular change was ostensibly part of an overall improvement to the existing

design, it seems likely that the new undercarriage arrangement was a symptom of Avro's desire to export the Shackleton, and it was clear that the better visibility and handling qualities afforded by tricycle undercarriage would make the aircraft a more viable export product (the SAAF had already raised this issue with Avro). However, tricycle undercarriage required the installation of a nose wheel assembly and this necessitated a redesign of the forward fuselage and lower nose section, including changes to the proportions of the bomb bay (enabling Avro to improve bomb loading procedures) and this, combined with the redesigned outer wings, created an aircraft that was strikingly different to the Shackleton Mk.2 and much heavier – estimated at 100,000lb. Avro proposed that the company should finance development of the aircraft if the RAF would order at least 30 airframes, on the assumption that further aircraft would be sold for export.

It is important to understand that by 1952 the RAF's procurement plans were very different to those that had been laid-out in advance of the Shackleton's original design and development. The need for rapid expansion in the face of the growing Cold

War threat from the Soviet Union led to a greater and urgent demand for maritime patrol aircraft, and Britain's political position was also changing significantly and swiftly. These factors had a direct effect on the Air Ministry's requirements and directly affected the Shackleton programme. As described previously, the Shackleton proved itself to be a robust and relatively reliable machine but one that consistently failed to meet the performance requirements that had been demanded of it. In other circumstances it is quite likely that the Shackleton would have been abandoned after production of the first Mk.1 variant, but with an urgent need for more and more maritime patrol aircraft, the Shackleton was in effect the only design that was available. The Air Staff's plan to develop a new flying boat to replace the RAF's elderly Sunderlands was eventually abandoned when it eventually became accepted that the need for a flying boat was no longer of such importance as Britain gradually withdrew from its commitments in the "East of Suez" region. It was former Coastal Command AOC-in-C Sir John Slessor who finally questioned whether the proposed project was worthwhile when it might result in a squadron of little more than five aircraft

Christmas Island was the site for testing British thermonuclear weapons in a phased programme, which lasted two and a half years. Shackleton squadrons were involved in every phase, performing roles that included patrols of the prohibited areas, meteorological reconnaissance, SAR and casualty evacuation, and regular transport shuttles between Christmas Island and Honolulu. After an initial detachment by two 206 Squadron aircraft from St.Eval, all three Ballykelly squadrons bore the brunt of the work until the completion of the tests in late 1958. Aircraft participating in Grapple wore special markings consisting of a large red frigate bird clutching a grappling hook placed above a union flag outlined in white. A number of aircraft were also modified to carry monitoring devices and atomic particle sensors. *(Photos: Ashley Annis & Tim McLelland collection)*

WR957 is pictured at Ballykelly whilst assigned to 204 Squadron early in 1961. During April of that year the aircraft was involved in a night flying exercise and struck the sea surface, causing extensive damage to the aircraft's lower fuselage, bomb bay and radar cupola. Repairs were completed at Ballykelly and the aircraft returned to service with 204 Squadron until March 1967 when it was withdrawn pending disposal. *(Photo: Tim Mclelland collection)*

WR954 is pictured during 1970 just a few eeks before the aircraft reached retirement. Assigned to 205 squadron in Singapore, the aircraft was ferried back to the UK on 17 September, and placed in open storage until May 1973 when it was scrapped on site. *(Photo: Tim McLelland collection)*

WL745 is pictured at Gan during 1962 when the aircraft was operated by 205 Squadron. After suffering two accidents, the aircraft was repaired on both occasions and returned to the UK for conversion to Phase III standard in November 1965, joining 204 Squadron upon completion. It was then transferred to HAS at Woodford during March 1970 to become a trials aircraft for the AEW programme. *(Photo: Ashley Annis collection)*

WG555 is seen at RAF Finningley's Battle of Britain At Home day on 19 September 1964, sharing the display site with a Voodoo, Varsity, Victor, and resident Vulcans. Wearing the markings of No.204 squadron, the aircraft flew over from Ballykelly to attend the show. *(Photo: Tony Clarke collection)*

assigned to the Far East. He asked whether "our survival in the early stages or our ability to win a future war depend on having a big, long range flying boat?" The Air Staff eventually resolved to allow the Sunderland to quietly be phased out of service by the end of 1958, stipulating that any aircraft that became unserviceable would not be repaired so that any further additional spending could be allocated elsewhere. Having originally built the Sunderland, the government-owned Shorts company was destined to create the RAF's new flying boat, but when the project was finally dropped, there was obvious political concern that Shorts would struggle to survive, and one Air Ministry memo addresses the issue of whether it would be possible to "find enough work to keep them

usefully employed." Consequently, the Air Ministry revisited the question of whether a short-range maritime patrol aircraft should be procured, not least because the American-supplied Neptunes were clearly on a par with the Shackleton in terms of range capability, therefore a shorter-range aircraft was still seen as a plausible option, even if it wasn't exactly vital for the RAF's future needs. The result was a decision to build a batch of 30 Seamews for the RAF. The Seamew was designed by Shorts as a replacement for the Grumman Avenger, assigned to the Fleet Air Arm's reserve squadrons. This unusual machine (at least in its prototype form) demonstrated some alarming and potentially lethal handling characteristics, and the Navy eventually lost interest in the aircraft, leaving

the RAF to accept a naval aircraft with folding wings, a tail hook and equipment that was largely unsuitable for the short-range land-based maritime role. Thankfully, sanity eventually prevailed and the Treasury refused to finance the Seamew, enabling the RAF to look at other options.

It is probably fair to say that the short-range maritime aircraft requirement was never a particularly important issue, as both medium and long range aircraft were perfectly capable of performing shorter missions when necessary, albeit at greater cost. Eventually, it was the American decision to refuse the supply of more Neptunes (for Nos.37 and 38 Squadrons in the Mediterranean) that forced the RAF to consider buying more Shackletons. It had been decided that when fully equipped the RAF's maritime force should consist of 11 squadrons, operating a total of 88 aircraft. The prospect of attrition losses combined with a necessary reserve of 13 airframes meant that by March 1954 the force would slowly fall below its full strength figure and front-line capability would be affected unless more aircraft were brought into service. The Ministry of Supply was reluctant to embrace Avro's new Shackleton MR. Mk.2A as a solution, believing that the additional Shackleton MR.Mk.2 aircraft would be adequate for maintaining an acceptable level of capability. The MoS estimated that the Mk.2A would weigh at least 102,000lb and its take-off performance would be marginal at best, while asymmetric handling would probably be unacceptably poor. By November 1952 Avro had responded with figures that confirmed the

aircraft's weight at 98,000lb with a range of 2,600nm, while the take-off performance remained unchanged, although it was estimated that in tropical conditions a take-off run of 6,300ft would be needed to clear a 50ft perimeter obstacle. The Air Ministry was unconvinced, but grudgingly it was agreed that the Mk.2A could be adopted, if it met Avro's predicted performance figures, even though this might require some sort of assisted take-off equipment for tropical operations (the standard airfield runway length was 6,000ft). The draft Operational requirement OR.320 (which had been in existence in one form or another since 1947) was re-written to meet the specifications of the projected Shackleton MR.Mk.2A, neatly reversing the standard procurement process in which the manufacturer was supposed to create an aircraft to meet the customer's

specifications. But the Air Ministry had no other alternative if it was to acquire more aircraft as swiftly as possible. Bristol proposed a maritime derivative of its new Britannia airliner and this was judged by the Air Ministry to be a superior machine, but the time and cost involved in creating a completely new aircraft was prohibitive and the revised OR.320 document reluctantly stated that the new Shackleton variant represented "the cheapest and quickest solution".

The Air Ministry's revised plans called for a total of 180 Shackletons to be in service and this meant some 16 additional aircraft beyond those already contracted. Avro had already specified that a minimum of 30 aircraft would be necessary, therefore the MoS reluctantly ordered 41 aircraft, provided that 25 aircraft from the existing Mk.2 production programme could be

WR966 was operated by Nos. 220, 228, 37, 204 and 210 squadrons before being converted to T.Mk.2 trainer configuration. After spending some time with MOTU and 236 OCU it was reconfigured as a standard MR.Mk.2 airframe and joined 205 Squadron at Changi. When it returned to the UK for storage pending disposal in January 1972 it had received some unusual "farewell" markings, including "White Knuckle Airlines" titling and an additional "T" code on its nose. Sadly, the bizarre markings didn't last long and the aircraft was scrapped at St.Athan during June 1973. (Photo: Ashley Annis collection)

cancelled (this was later reduced to 20). Avro accepted the order without further negotiation, not least because the company was eager to forge ahead with the new variant in response to interest emerging from South Africa for an export version of the aircraft. Indeed, Avro had already started work on the project as a private venture, anticipating with remarkable confidence that the RAF would eventually order the aircraft. The RAF certainly had more than a few misgivings but with no other realistic option on the table, the Shackleton MR.Mk.3 was born. The MoS estimated that the new Shackleton variant wouldn't not be ready for service entry until June 1955 and by this stage the Operational Requirement had been modified to reflect this, and also introduced some new stipulations such as the ability to operate over the Indian Ocean (something that was relevant to both the

RAF and South African Air Force), a fatigue life of at least 10,000 hours, a take-off distance of 5,250ft or less (to clear 50ft), provision for flight refueling, and improvements to the crew stations, systems and armament options. The MoS also requested Treasury approval to acquire 22 Mk.3 Shackletons to replace the remaining MR.Mk.1 aircraft that were still with front-line squadrons, allowing these to be shifted to training duties. But as development of the Shackleton Mk.3 continued through 1953, the Air Ministry still refused to place a firm order, and Avro struggled to continue financing the project without any firm prospect of recovering the cost, and it was becoming clear that a break would have to be made between completion of Mk.2 aircraft and commencement of Mk.3 production, creating even most expense. As the Mk.3

mock-up slowly assembled, there were many aspects of the design that had to be revised in response to the RAF's reservations, such as the position of the nose escape hatch, the position of control selectors in the cockpit, and the inadequacy of the air conditioning system. But overall the new design seemed satisfactory, particularly the new Tactical station, the improved galley and rest area, and the new cockpit canopy, complete with a central escape hatch that could be opened on the ground for ventilation. At long last (and partly in response to SAAF requirements) the Shackleton would finally afford some comfort to the crew members with new armchair-style seats, a wardroom with six bunks, better soundproofing and even a toilet compartment. Externally, the new nose section incorporated the new nose wheel assembly, a new autolycus system,

A magnificent air-to-air view of a 42 Squadron Shackleton, illustrating the aircraft's upper wing surfaces. In addition to the usual national insignia roundels, Shackletons carried wing walkway markings painted in yellow, indicating the inner portions of the structure that were sufficiently robust to withstand the weight of ground crew. *(Photo: Aeroplane)*

stowage for sonobuoys and flare chutes. During September Contract 6/Acft/6408/CB.6(a) was issued to cover 17 new aircraft, together with arrangements to complete the last 20 Mk.2 aircraft to Mk.3 standard.

As ever, the Air Ministry and Ministry of Supply began to make changes to specifications almost immediately after the new contract was signed. A new TKS aerofoil anti-icing system was stipulated and this required structural alterations that affected both cost and production time scale. The new twin mainwheel assemblies were to be fixed to the aircraft's rear spar, and this necessitated some modifications to the shape of the inner engine nacelle fairings, as these would also now be expected to accommodate a rocket motor for take-off boost in tropical conditions. Avro preferred a Napier liquid-fuelled motor for this facility but the MoS insisted on the deHavilland Scarab solid fuel motor that was also expected to be fitted to the Beverley transport, and the issue remained unresolved for some time. The airborne lifeboat that had first been proposed for earlier Shackleton variants was reintroduced, even though it was accepted that this would create yet more delays. Likewise, the nose gun installation for the Mk.2 was also stipulated for the Mk.3, even though the new aircraft would not have

A rare image of a Shackleton MR.Mk.2 "in action" albeit for public display purposes, as a 42 squadron machine deposits dummy depth charges during an Air Show in Malta. *(Photo: Godfrey Mangion)*

cockpit side windows to open when the guns were fired. More constructively, the Griffon engine's exhaust pipe was finally accepted for use on the new aircraft and it was eventually retrofitted to many existing Mk.2 machines at a later stage. Other changes were also made to the Tactical station, additional navigation equipment was introduced and plans for a

new launch chute were discussed, as well as the installation of a new periscope sextant. Although no major changes where proposed, the growing list of relatively minor alterations served to delay the new type's completion, and the question of delivery dates finally came to a head when Avro announced that the first full production-standard Mk.3 aircraft

No.210 Squadron acquired Shackletons on 1 december 1958 when the unit adopted No.269 Squadron's number and assumed control of that unit's aircraft. Based at Ballykelly, the unit moved to Sharjah, Oman, during November 1970 and remained there until November of the following year when the squadron disbanded. As can be seen, the unit applied its squadron emblem on a white circle, applied on the aircraft's nose. WL748 joined 210 Squadron in 1961, moving to the RRE at Pershore after conversion to Phase III standard in 1967. *(Photo: Tim McLelland collection)*

WB833 was the Shackleton MR.Mk.2 prototype, assigned to trials and evaluation work until November 1960 when it joined the ASWDU at Ballykelly (as illustrated). After modification to Phase III standard the aircraft was issued to 210 squadron (now coded T). It crashed on the Mull of Kintrye on 19 April 1968 in foul weather conditions. *(Photo: Tim McLelland collection)*

RAF Ballykelly boasted a particularly unusual runway arrangement thanks to the local railway network. The Londonderry rail tracks crossed the runway (or to be more precise, the runway crossed the railway after it was extended during the 1940s) and aircraft were required to give-way to railway trains, causing some interesting moments for Air Traffic Control. This picture illustrates the crossing of the last steam engine to use the network while a Shackleton crew wait patiently. *(Photo: Tim Mclelland collection)*

WL759 served with Nos. 37 and 204 squadrons before joining 38 Squadron in March 1959. It moved to Singapore as a Phase II aircraft in August 1966 and eventually became the last Phase II aircraft to operate with that unit. It participated in the squadron's "farewell" formation flypast on 8 November 1968 before being withdrawn from use three days later. Destined to remain in Singapore, the aircraft was broken-up and scrapped on site at Changi in 1969.

would go to South Africa, now that a contract had been signed for supply of aircraft to the SAAF. Not surprisingly, the Air Ministry objected to the prospect of taking second place to an export customer and, much to both the RAF's and Avro's surprise, the SAAF agreed to accept the 10th and 11th new airframes as their first deliveries. But even as this issue was resolved, the Air Ministry and MoS had become increasingly concerned that the Shackleton Mk.3 would not meet its predicted performance figures.

The predicted take-off performance figure of 5,250ft was soon regarded as unachievable at weights above 90,000lb and that the aircraft's poor rate of climb following an engine failure would be unacceptable. Some form of assisted take-off equipment would be vital if the aircraft was to operate from standard 6,000ft runways in hot and high conditions. Conventional jet engines such as the Soar and Viper were examined but they were judged to be insufficiently powerful, whereas the new Super Sprite rocket was too heavy to carry on the aircraft centerline, and placing a motor on each wing would provide too much thrust. The Scarab motor appeared to be the logical choice but no decision was made. The aircraft's predicted range was also gradually decreasing as the aircraft's weight increased and when Avro concluded that the aircraft would be able to maintain a patrol of little more than two hours at a range of 1,000nm, the Air Ministry concluded that the prospect of closing the mid-Atlantic gap was still as unlikely as it had been many years previously. Officials within the RAF, Air Ministry and MoS pressed for the Shackleton Mk.3 programme to be cancelled, but the Air Ministry's Operational Requirements branch maintained that the Shackleton Mk.3 was the only available option unless the RAF was to continue operating only the Shackleton Mk.2 for many more years. It also seemed inevitable that if the RAF pulled out, the SAAF order would also have to be abandoned, therefore development of the Mk.3 continued, even though by this stage the RAF didn't really want it.

Possibly the most unusual Shackleton MR.Mk.2 was WG557, which was delivered to 206 Squadron in February 1953 after making its first flight on 5 November 1952. It was damaged on 10 December 1953 when its tail wheel collapsed on landing but after repairs it returned to the unit before joining 220 Squadron on 19 March 1954, followed by 228 Squadron on 16 September. After some time in storage it was allocated to the Royal Aircraft Establishment as a replacement for the Armament Flight's Lincoln. It arrived at Farnborough on 20 December 1957 and transferred to the Empire Test Pilots School on 29 September 1960 (although it returned to the Armament Flight for underwater data transmission trials). It was repainted with the grey and white colour positions reversed, combined with red serials. As part of the Armament Flight trials the aircraft also received "Royal Navy" titling. (Photo: Aeroplane)

On 2 September 1955 the MR.Mk.3 prototype (WR970) made its first flight and quickly completed ten hours of flying in order to appear at the SBAC Farnborough show a couple of days later. Devoid of most of the planned internal equipment, the aircraft participated in the show's flying programme, but was found to have suffered wing skin buckling during its performances. This disturbing development resulted in the aircraft returning to Woodford for wing stiffness and resonance testing and by the end of the year the outer wings had been refitted with thicker (and therefore heavier) metal. This worrying episode was enough to convince the RAF that assisted take-off was a potentially troublesome option that would be best avoided, and it was accepted that the aircraft would simply have to operate at lighter weights in tropical conditions. It was also enough to prompt the MoS to reduce the Mk.3 order from a total of 50 aircraft to just 34. As flight testing got underway, WR970 was operated at increasing weights up to 92,000lb, but after the 21st flight yet more skin buckling was discovered, this time on the rear fuselage. Repairs were swiftly undertaken but just four flights later the centre section root ribs were found to have partially sheared. Excessive movenet in the outer engine mountings had also caused skin cracking, and WR970 was again laid-up for yet more strengthening. Sadly, the Shackleton's problems were far from over, and the failure of the test specimen's nose structure on 3 May (during nose wheel testing) was only one of many problems that arose, leading Coastal Command's Commander-in-Chief to express concern that the front-line strength would be lost in 1957 if new Shackleton's could not be delivered as promised. Avro switched to a 24-hour work shift programme and a second Shackleton Mk.3 (WR971) took to the air on 28 May. This was to have been swiftly followed by WR972 just a few weeks later, but a two-month industrial strike by Avro workers brought almost all activity to a halt during the summer of 1956 and it wasn't until 6 November that the aircraft completed its maiden flight.

T.Mk.2 WR966 is pictured at Kinloss during June 1970 whilst assigned to 236 Operational Conversion Unit (formerly MOTU). Shortly after this photo was taken it was converted back to MR.Mk.2 standard with Phase III modifications. It was transferred to 205 Squadron on 19 January 1971 coded G, and subsequently joined 204 squadron's Far East detachment. It remained with that unit until Nimrods arrived as replacements, flying to St.Athan on 10 January 1972 for storage. It was dismantled and removed on 22 June 1973. *(Photo: Ashley Annis)*

MR.Mk.2 WR961 was formerly with 228, 224, 37 and 38 Squadrons and finally the Ballykelly Wing in 1968 before moving to HAS Bitteswell for modifications, after which it was assigned to 204 Squadron in October 1970. It joined the Majunga Detachment Support Unit on 31 March 1971 and remained there until 19 April 1972 when it was flown to Kemble and placed in storage (as illustrated). It remained here until 1 January 1978 when it was dismantled and removed as scrap. *(Photo: Ashley Annis)*

Flight testing revealed various problems with the aircraft, but nothing unusual for what was in affect a new design. Aileron flutter and airframe resonance required more time to resolve, as did the aircraft's excessively heavy stick forces, and with development of the Vulcan bomber now taking priority at Woodford, the Shackleton project team struggled. The Mk.3's stall characteristics were found to be far from satisfactory, and although a tendency to roll in the stall was cured, the aircraft still exhibited aileron snatching and considerable pitching. Worse still, the buffet warning manifested itself only two knots before the actual stall, and in order to make the aircraft more acceptable for evaluation by A&AEE pilots at Boscombe Down, an artificial stall

warning device was installed on WR970. Additional strengthening was also undertaken in anticipation of trials at weights up to 100,000lb and this delayed the aircraft's arrival at Boscombe Down, where test pilots reported that overall handling was acceptable, even though the stall warning device was "useless" and the aircraft's stall characteristics (in attack configuration) were "vicious." AOC-in-C Coastal Command flew the aircraft and expressed satisfaction in the greatly improved crew environment, even though he remained guarded about his opinion of the aircraft's performance. The Mk.3's violent stall characteristics were still being investigated on 7 December when Squadron Leader Jack Wales (part of Avro's production test team) embarked on a test

flight from Woodford. The crew of a Lincoln bomber reported seeing the Shackleton enter into a spin at around 6,000ft before disappearing into cloud and WR970 was next seen above the village of Foolow in Derbyshire, flying slowly in a rapid descent. The aircraft crashed and cartwheeled before bursting into flames, killing all on board. Investigations revealed that the aircraft's engines had failed due to the presence of engine oil in the manifolds, this being caused by the aircraft flying inverted. The aircraft had been in a climbing turn with bomb doors open (the aircraft's attack configuration) and despite recovering from the inverted attitude whilst in cloud, the failed engines sealed the aircraft's fate. Naturally, the crash delayed the Mk.3 programme even further but WR971

Shackleton MR.Mk.2 (formerly a T.Mk.2) WR969 is pictured at St.Athan during 1972, after having returned from Singapore during the previous September. With wing tips and engines removed, the aircraft remained here until July 1974 when it was dismantled and removed as scrap. *(Photo: Ashley Annis)*

◄ WL751 first flew on 5 March 1953, joining 224 Squadron during May of that year. It received Phase III modifications in 1966 and then went to HAS for trials work with stall warning devices. After serving with the Majunga Detachment Support Unit, the aircraft returned to its parent unit (204 Squadron) at Honington during February 1972 and was struck off charge on 4 May when it flew to Baginton. After its owner (Shackleton Aviation) moved, the aircraft was acquired by HAS pending resale in the USA but it was subsequently abandoned at Coventry and scrapped on site during January 1975. As illustrated, the aircraft carried an orange band across its fuselage, applied for identification purposes during an exercise in 1960. *(Photo: Ashley Annis)*

◄ Pictured in 1962 whilst operating with 224 Squadron, WL789 was previously used for MAD trials, fitted with a Magnetic Anomaly Detector boom whilst assigned to the ASWDU at St.Mawgan. It joined 38 Squadron in October 1966 and transferred to 205 Squadron coded H in January 1967. It returned to the UK in August 1967, to be placed in storage at Shawbury pending disposal. It was scrapped on site in March 1969. *(Photo: Tim McLelland collection)*

A rural scene at Ballykelly, showing Shackleton MR.Mk.2 WG533 from No.224 Squadron in 1963, complete with Royal Air Force titling and the unit's badge on the aircraft's nose. WG533 played an interesting part in the Shackleton's story, having been assigned to the RAF Handling Squadron at Manby, where the aircraft's "Pilot's Notes" manual was compiled. *(Photo: Ashley Annis)*

finally arrived at Boscombe Down on 14 December, followed by WR972 a couple of weeks later.

WR973 (the fourth Mk.3) resumed the aircraft's stall warning tests while the fifth aircraft was allocated to tropical trials, although completion of this and the sixth aircraft was delayed because of Avro's need to comply with contractual arrangements that had been made with South Africa for production of its batch of Shackletons. Oddly, while two aircraft were at Boscombe Down awaiting CA Release, the SAAF would not officially accept their aircraft until a British CA Release had been obtained, and so a bizarre cycle of delay ensued, until an initial CA Release was finally issued on 24 April 1957. Performance was still judged to be disappointing, and Rolls-Royce embarked upon a modification programme to tweak additional power out of the Griffon 57 engine, resulting in an additional 145hp. This encouraging development was offset by the news that fatigue testing showed the aircraft would have a fatigue life of only 3,600 hours. Avro was somewhat embarrassed by this finding, and immediately assured the Air Ministry that yet more structural modifications would extend this figure by a considerable amount, but it did little to improve the RAF's enthusiasm for the aircraft, and the Shackleton Mk.3 officially entered RAF service on 30 August 1957, when WR976 joined No.220 Squadron at St.Mawgan with little fuss or fanfare. By this stage the first SAAF aircraft had arrived in South Africa, the first two aircraft (1716 and 1717) having been officially handed over on 24 April at

Baking in the sun on the ramp at RAF Luqa, WG555 is pictured during October 1969 whilst assigned to No.204 squadron. In 1971 the aircraft was transferred to the Majunga Detachment Support Unit and remained there until February 1972 when it completed the long journey back to 204 Squadron's headquarters that were then at Honington. It made its last flight on 9 May 1972 when it was ferried to RAF Catterick for ground use by the RAF Fire Fighting School. It was removed as scrap some years later. *(Photo: Ashley Annis)*

Woodford. Five days later these (plus 1718) were flown to RAF St.Mawgan in Cornwall to enable SAAF crews to train on the aircraft in co-operation with their RAF counterparts, whilst participating in joint exercises with the Royal Navy. Nobody could have failed to notice the absurdity of the new Shackleton variant having been delivered to the SAAF before the RAF, but the responsibility for this situation lay firmly in the hands of the RAF and Avro, and the SAAF appeared to be satisfied with the aircraft that they had purchased, even though it's introduction

was marred by yet more skin cracking which prompted the SAAF to temporarily ground the aircraft at St.Mawgan while an Avro working party rectified the problem. These three aircraft arrived at Ysterplaat near Capetown on 18 August and were followed by the remaining five examples over successive weeks, the last (1723) arriving on 26 February 1958. Inevitably, a number of technical issued soon arose, including unexpected losses of engine power that were traced to air entering the aircraft's fuel system through the tank

vents. Hydraulic failures were also common because of piping that wasn't strong enough to handle the aircraft's increased pressures. The new nose wheel undercarriage assembly also caused many problems, its locking mechanism proving troublesome, and the entire assembly could sometimes refuse to extend, or collapse on landing, leaving the huge former "tail dragger" in a precarious tail-up attitude with the entrance door some thirty feet above ground, forcing the crew to leave the aircraft via the over-wing escape hatch. ❖

The prototype Shackleton MR.Mk.1 made its first flight on 2 September 1955, appearing at the SBAC Farnborough show a few days later. It was assigned to A&AEE Boscombe Down for handling trials and used by Avro for development and evaluation work, including a great deal of stall warning investigations. It was this issue that was being explored on 7 December 1956 when the aircraft crashed in Derbyshire, killing all on board. The aircraft had stalled and entered a spin whilst set-up in "attack" configuration with the bomb bay doors open and radome extended — a situation in which Boscombe Down's pilots had found the aircraft to possess violent stall characteristics. Test Pilot Squadron Leader Wales managed to recover from the spin whilst in cloud but the aircraft had become inverted during recovery manoeuvres, and this had led to engine failure, and with a significant rate of descent already affecting the aircraft, it was impossible to recover the aircraft within the limited amount of height that was still available. This tragic beginning to the MR3 programme didn't have a long-term effect on progress, as the incident was not attributed to any deficiencies, although the Mk.3's stall characteristics were never improved significantly. Various attempts were made to install effective stall warning devices. *(Photos: Aeroplane)*

Avro Shackleton
Data

POWER PLANTS

Four 12-cylinder, pressure liquid-cooled, two-speed, single-stage supercharged
Rolls-Royce Griffon engines producing 1960 hp (2435 hp with water methanol)
at maximum power.

Griffon Variants

MR.Mk.1/T.Mk.4	MR.Mk.2	MR.Mk.2 Phase I/II	MR.Mk.3 Phase III	MR.Mk.3* Ph IIII	AEW/T.Mk.2 Phase III
57/57A	57A/57A	58	57A	58	58

*plus two 2500lb thrust Rolls-Royce Viper 203 power plants.

PROPELLERS

De Havilland 13 ft-diameter counter-rotating, constant-speed, fully feathering units.

FRONT: Left-hand tractor DF 1 60/3 34/1 or DB 171/334/1
with basic setting a fine pitch 23degrees, feathered 90degrees.

REAR: Right-hand tractor DF 1 60/336/1 or DB 171/336/1
with basic setting and fine pitch 24degrees, feathered 91degrees.

FUEL SYSTEM

AvGas 100/ 130 NATO F-18.
Tank Capacities (gallons)

	MR.Mk.1/T.Mk.4	MR.Mk.2 Phase I/II	MR.Mk.2 Phase III
Tank 1	2 x 497	2 x 497	2 x 497
2	2 x 541	2 x 541	2 x 570
3	2 x 297	2 x 297	2 x 297
4	2 x 311	2 x 311	2 x 311
5			
Totals*	3292	3292	3350

	T.Mk.2/AEW	MR.Mk.3 Phase 1/11	MR.MK.3 Phase III
Tank 1	2 x 497	2 x 539	2 x 539
2	2 x 570	2 x 541	2 x 573
3	2 x 297	2 x 297	2 x 297
4	2 x 3 a11	2 x 311	2 x 311
-		2 x 185	2 x 185
6 (tip)		2 x 251**	2 x 253**
Totals*	3350	248	4316

  * all variants could carry 400 gal auxiliary tanks in the bomb bay.
** wing-tip tanks nominally 256 gal but actual capacity varied.

PERFORMANCE

	MR.Mk.1/T.Mk.4	MR.Mk.2	MR.Mk.2 Phase III	AEW.Mk.2	MR.Mk.3*
Max speed @ 12,000 ft**	294	299	286	262	297
Max cruise @ 10,000 ft **	245	249	249	-	253
Long-range cruise	180-200 mph depending on weight @1500 5000ft				
Landing speed**	114	114	116	116	118
Stalling speed**	88	88	92	92	96
Initial rate of climb (ft/min)	1,005	920	900	900	850
Initial rate of climb (3 engine)(ft/min)	592	495	463	460	200
Ceiling (ft)	20,700	20,200	18,800	-	18,600
Range (nm)***	2,160	1,980	1,720	-	2,300
Radius of 4 hr patrol (nm)	780	700	670	-	970
Endurance (hrs) (20% reserve)	14.8	14.6	13	13	16
Max still air range (nm)	3,090	2,900	2,780	2,700	1,660

ato 50ft using Water Methanol
Mk.3 Phase III (Viper) had improved take off performance (4,750 ft to clear 50 ft screen), but reduced range and endurance. ** speeds in mph.
*** at 5,000ft at 190 mph (full load - 20% reserve)

DIMENSIONS (ft)

	MR.Mk.1/T.Mk.4	MR.Mk.2	MR.Mk.3
Wing span	120	120	119.83
Length	77.5	87.3	87.3
Height	17.5	17.5	23.35
Tailplane span	33	33	33
Wheel track	23.75	23.75	23.75

AREAS (sq ft)

	MR.Mk.1/T.Mk.4	MR.Mk.2	MR.Mk.3
Wing (inc. ailerons)	1421	1421	1458
Ailerons	110.1	110.1	133.4
Flaps	146.96	146.96	146.96
Tailplane (inc. elevators)	285.4	285.4	285.4
Elevators	87.3	87.3	87.3
Fins	116	116	116
Rudders	106.4	106.4	106.4

WEIGHTS (lb)

	MR.Mk.1/T.Mk.4	MR.Mk.2	MR.Mk.2/T.Mk.2 Phase III
Empty	49,600*	51,400	59,000
Loaded (normal)	82,000	84,000	89,000
Loaded (max T/0)	86,000**	86,000	95,500
Landing (normal)	72,000	72,000	80,000
Stores load (with full fuel)	Approximately 6000 lb		
Stores load (max)	12,000	15,000	15,000

	AEW.Mk.2	MR.Mk. 3	MR.Mk.3 Phase III (Viper)
Empty	58,800	57,800	64,300
Loaded (normal)	89,000	85,000	95,000
Loaded (max T/0)	96,100	100,000	108,000***
Landing (normal)	80,000	86,000	88,000

Stores load Approximately 6000 lb (with full fuel) stores load 12,000

* Phase II T.Mk.4 54,500 lb   ** Grapple aircraft 87,500 lb
*** MR.Mk.3 Phase III (non-Viper) 104,000 lb

All information supplied courtesy John Botwood (www.avroshackleton.com)

AVRO SHACKLETON
IN DETAIL

Shackleton AEW.Mk.2 WL754 pictured shortly
before the aircraft was retired in January 1981.
Its final flight was to RAF Valley on 22 January,
after which efforts were made to retain the
aircraft for public display, allocated as 8665M.
sadly, the plans were abandoned and the aircraft
was eventually destroyed on Valley's fire dump.
(Photo: Aeroplane collection)

This series of images show a Shackleton MR.Mk.2 from No.42 Squadron, at RAF St.Eval. Of particular interest is the close-up look at the unmodified engine exhausts that were finally fitted with an exhaust pipe arrangement towards the end of the Mk.2's service life, as part of Phase II modification. *(Photos: Aeroplane collection)*

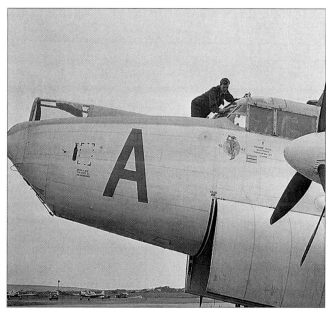

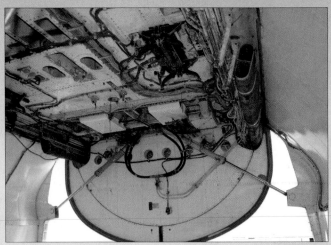

Close-up images of Shackleton WR963, a former MR.Mk.2 aircraft, converted to AEW.Mk.2 standard, and now partially reconverted to MR.Mk.2 status under the care of the Shackleton Preservation Trust. The SPT hope to restore the aircraft to flying condition if sufficient funds can be raised to conduct the necessary refurbishments, under the guidance of the Civil Aviation Authority and British Aerospace.

(Photos: Tim McLelland)

SQN LDR JOHN CUBBERLEY

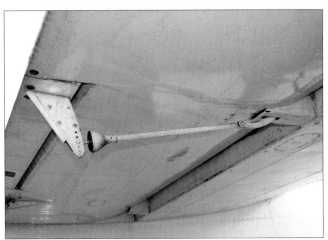

Close-up images of Shackleton WR963, currently on display at Coventry Airport. For the latest news on WR963, the Shackleton Preservation Trust can be found at www.avroshackleton.co.uk and on www.facebook.com/avro.shackleton

(Photo: Tim McLelland)

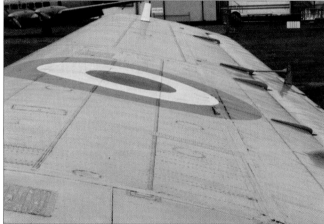

Detail images of the Shackleton Preservation Trust's WR963 at Coventry Airport showing the interior of the aircraft's wing flaps, bomb bay door, main undercarriage, engines and tail fin. *(Photos: Tim Mclelland)*

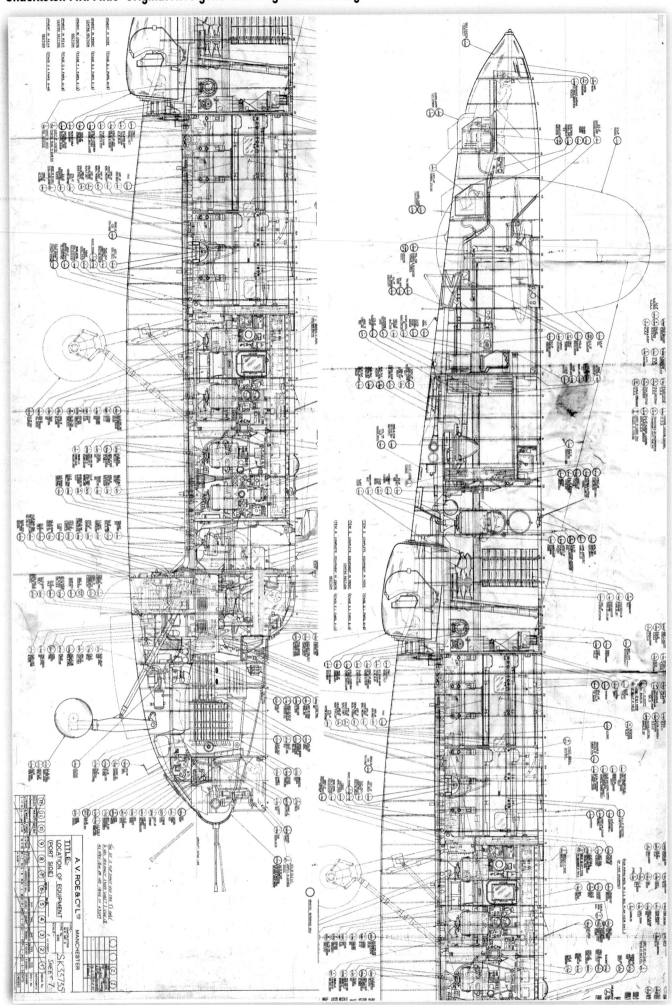

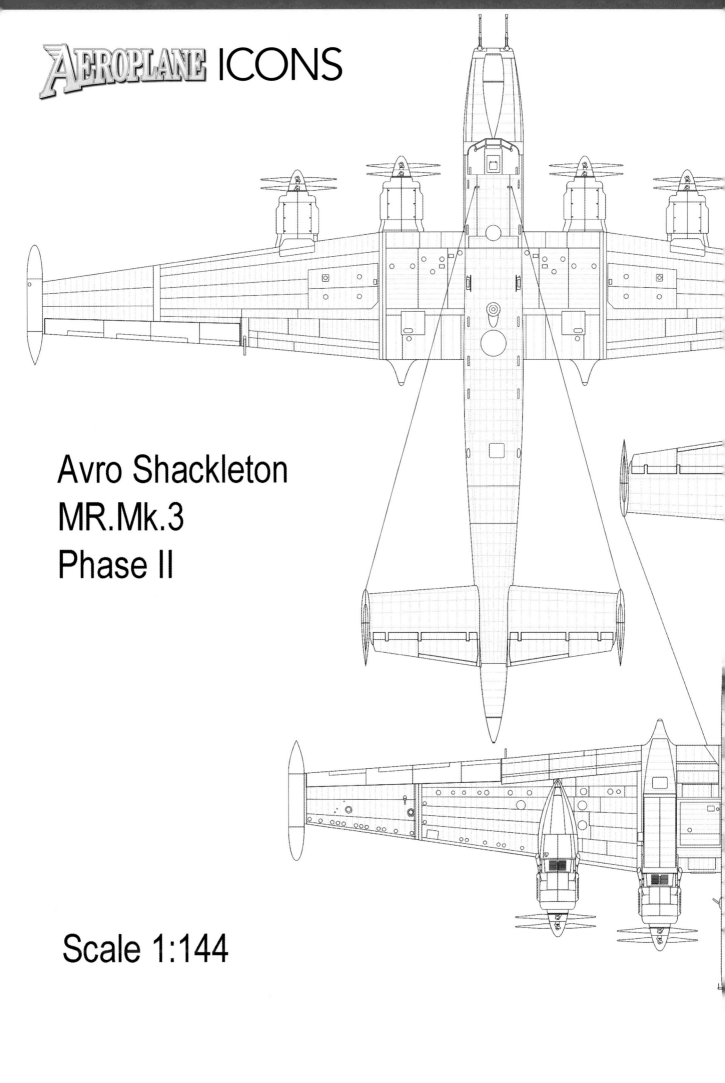

Avro Shackleton
MR.Mk.3
Phase II

Scale 1:144

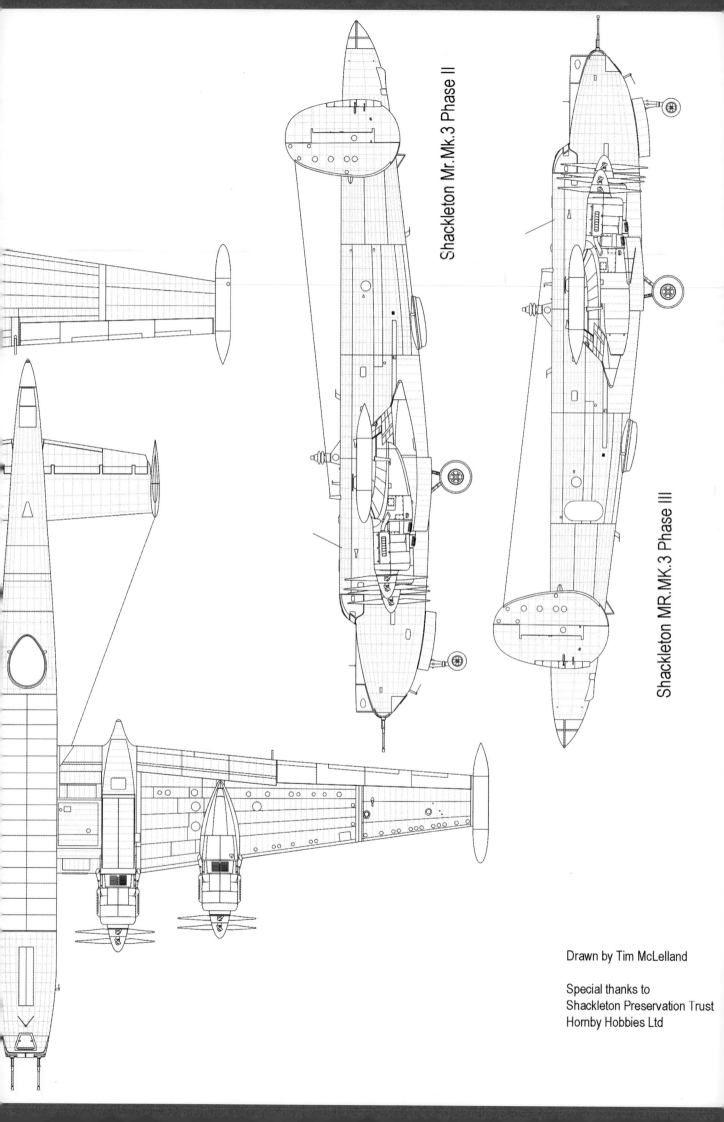

Shackleton Mr.Mk.3 Phase II

Shackleton MR.MK.3 Phase III

Drawn by Tim McLelland

Special thanks to
Shackleton Preservation Trust
Hornby Hobbies Ltd

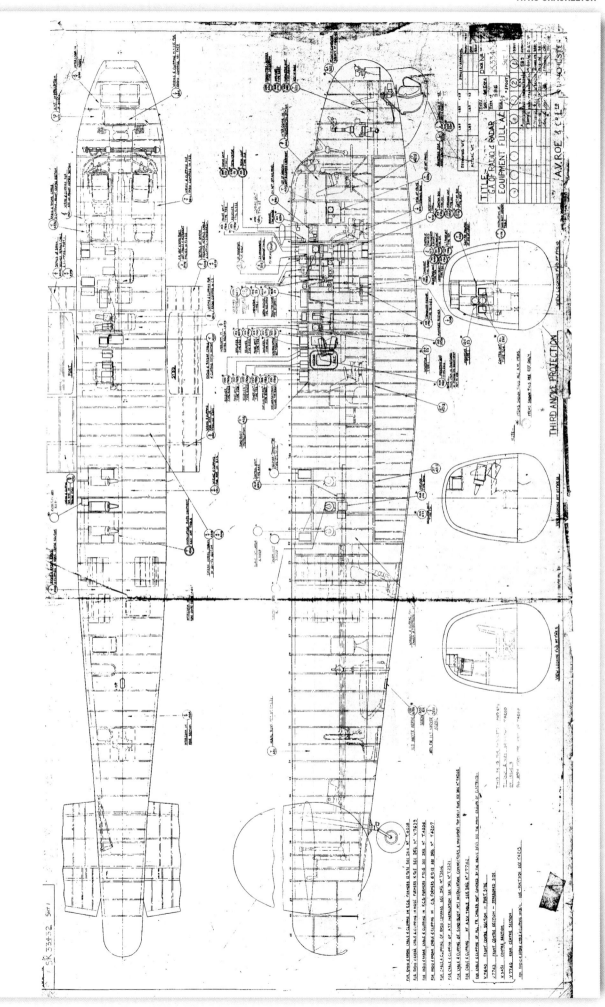

Interior views of Shackleton WR963. The aircraft retains most of the equipment installed for the Airborne Early Warning role, although the Shackleton Preservation Trust's volunteers are slowly re-equipping the aircraft with equipment from its maritime past. Most of the general internal structure and flight deck instrument layout has remained largely unchanged since the aircraft was manufactured in 1953. *(Photos: Tim Mclelland)*

Busy scene at Lossiemouth in No.8 Squadron's hangar. Not the crew hatch under the forward fuselage is removed. *(Photo: Aeroplane collection)*

Looking rearwards towards the tail of a Shackleton MR.Mk.1, with observer positions either side of the fuselage. The crew access door is open and the roof hatch is removed. *(Photo: Aeroplane)*

Shackleton AEW.Mk.2 forwar fuselage with radar gear removed. The support structure is visible, attached to the forward bomb bay area, with the forward section of the port bomb bay door attached. *(Photo: Tim McLelland collection)*

Mk.101 Lulu nuclear depth bomb and long range fuel tank, pictured in the bomb bay of a Shackleton MR.Mk.3. *(Photo: Tim McLelland collection)*

Shackleton MR.Mk.3 Phase II XF701, illustrating the Viper turbojet installation positioned behind the outer Griffon engine. The jet engine intake is in the closed position, under the nacelle. *(Photo: Aeroplane)*

Shackleton MR.Mk.3 Phase III XF708 pictured at the Imperial War Museum, Duxford, during restoration work that was conducted in 2014. With panels removed the relatively tiny Viper turbojet can be compared to the huge Griffon piston engine. *(Photos: David Whitworth)*

Two Mk.101 Lulu nuclear depth bombs either side of a single Mk.30 torpedo, in the bomb bay of a Shackleton Mk.3. *(Photo: Tim McLelland collection)*

Mk.101 Lulu nuclear depth bomb and a pair of Mk.30 homing torpedos and a K-type bomb trolley, under a Shackleton Mk.3. *(Photo: Tim McLelland collection)*

The American Mk.101 Lulu was supplied to the RAF for Shackletons as part of Project N, designated by the RAF as the Bomb, Aircraft, A, 1200lbs MC. Yeild was 11 kilotons. *(Photo: Tim McLelland collection)*

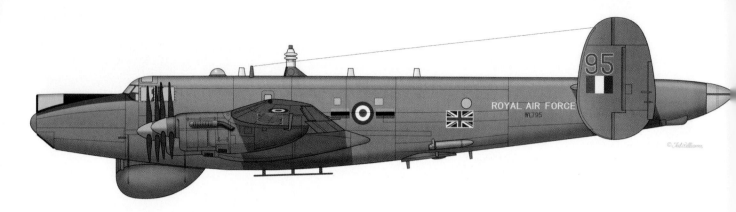

WL795 was manufactured as a Shackleton MR.Mk.2, delivered to the RAF (23 MU) on 8 September 1953. It was issued to 204 Squadron on 6 January 1954. It remained in service until February 1971 when it was placed in storage before being converted to AEW.Mk.2 standard. It joined No.8 Squadron late in 1972. It was retired on 24 November 1981 and flown to RAF St.Mawgan, where it is currently on display.

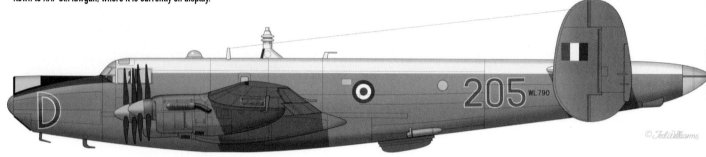

Shackleton MR.Mk.2 WL790 carries the markings of No.205 squadron, where it was assigned in June 1962. It was first coded E before being recoded D and retained this code after being modified to Phase III standard. It was withdrawn in January 1971 and joined 8 Squadron after being converted to AEW.Mk.2 standard late in 1972.

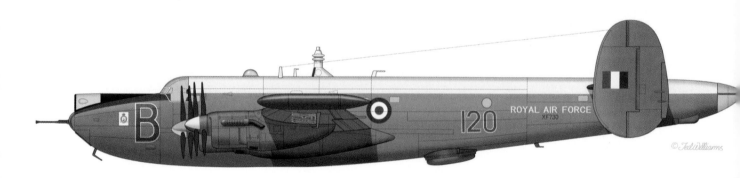

XF730 (Shackleton MR.Mk.3) was allocated to No.120 Squadron in December 1963, coded B, with the unit's badge applied on the aircraft's nose. It was subsequently upgrade to Phase III standard with Viper engines, and joined 42 Squadron until being withdrawn in June 1971 when it was ferried to Kinloss for use as a crash and rescue training airframe.

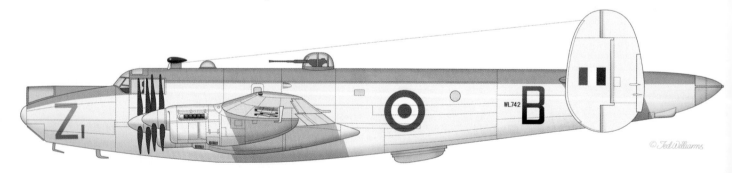

WL742 was delivered to the RAF as a Shackleton MR.Mk.2 on 4 February 1953. It was assigned to No.206 Squadron in March 1953 and received the codes B-Z as illustrated, the fuselage code applied in black and the nose code in Medium Sea Grey. It was withdrawn in February 1967 after operating with the Ballykelly Wing.

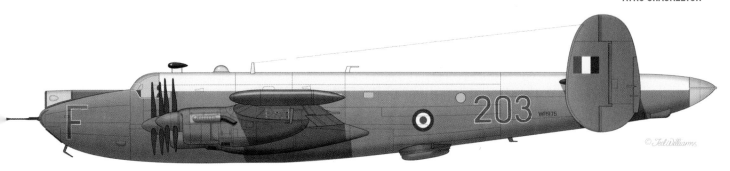

WR795 (Shackleton MR.MK.3) was issued to the RAF Handling Squadron during July 1957. It joined 220 Squadron in November 1957 coded P, in an overall Dark Sea Grey finish. After conversion to Phase II standard it joined 203 Squadron coded F as illustrated. After conversion to Phase III standard it joined the Kinloss Wing coded A and remained in service until 24 August 1970 when it was ferried to St.Athan.

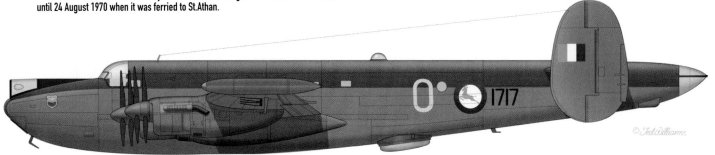

Shackleton MR.Mk.3 1717 made its first flight on 6 May 1957 and after training at St. Mawgan it flew to South Africa on 13 August 1957, joining No.35 Squadron SAAF. It was eventually upgraded to Phase III standard but Viper engines were not fitted to any of the SAAF aircraft. Re-sparred in 1977, the aircraft remained with 35 Squadron and was placed on display at the National Parks Board Museum before being broken up in 2009.

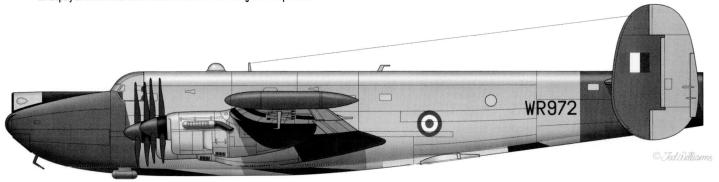

Shackleton MR.Mk.3 WR972 was assigned to the Royal Aircraft Establishment on parachute trials. Originally wearing standard grey and white colours, patches of fluorescent orange were applied to the aircraft, these being retained when the aircraft was later repainted silver (as illustrated). Undersides were painted with black and yellow stripes. The aircraft was later repainted in grey, white and blue RAE colours. The tail section was often removed for trials although an observation cupola could be fitted as required.

WR981 (Shackleton MR.Mk.3) wears the colours of No.206 Squadron, when the aircraft joined this unit at St.Mawgan during January 1958. It subsequently flew with 120 Squadron and then 203 squadron, coded E before rejoining 201 Squadron coded P. It returned to 120 Squadron coded B and then 201 Squadron coded N before finally joining the Kinloss Wing coded G, modified to Phase III standard. It was withdrawn on 27 November 1970.

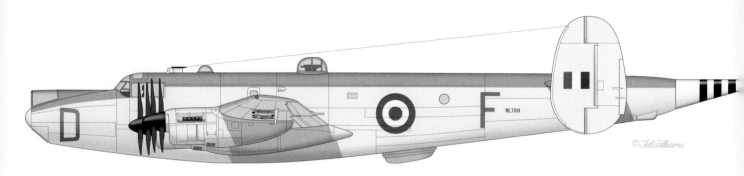

Shackleton MR.Mk.2 WL789 was delivered to No.38 MU at Llandow in July 1953, where it was fitted with a Magnetic Anomaly Detector tail boom for trials that were conducted from St.Mawgan. It remained on MAD trials until April 1958 by which stage the aircraft had been painted overall Dark Sea Grey, and the tail boom stripes had switched to red. After reverting to standard configuration the aircraft joined 224 Squadron and was retired in August 1967 after operating with 205 squadron at Changi.

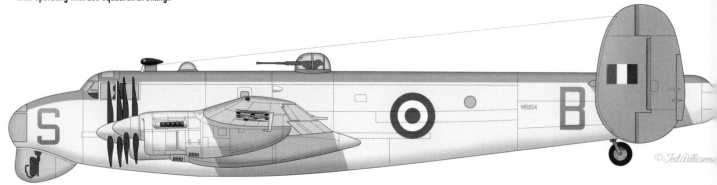

Shackleton MR.Mk.1 WB854 was issued to No.224 Squadron in April 1952 with the code B-S as illustrated. Unusually, the tail fins were painted Medium Sea Grey although a standard white finish was later applied. It was to have been modified to T.Mk.4 standard but this plan was abandoned and the aircraft went to Singapore, joining 205 Squadron in July 1958, coded C. After returning to the UK for re-sparring, it remained with 205 Squadron until 27 November 1962 when it was withdrawn and subsequently broken-up.

WR965 (Shackleton MR.Mk.2), assigned to No.37 Squadron based at Luqa. In addition to the standard unit markings, the aircraft wears black and yellow identification stripes, applied during the aircraft's participation in Operation Musketeer (the Suez Crisis). It is believed that some of the unit's aircraft may also have had stripes applied to wing surfaces. WR965 was subsequently converted to AEW.Mk.2 standard, and crashed on 30 April 1990 on the Hebrides in bad weather.

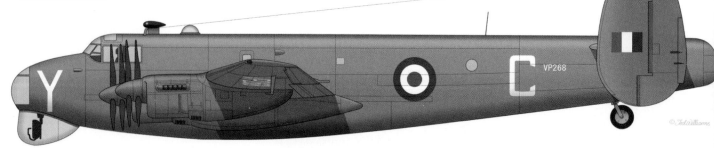

VP268 (Shackleton MR.Mk.1) made its first flight on 20 April 1951, joining No.236 Operational Conversion Unit at Kinloss on 15 July 1951, coded C-Y as illustrated. It remained with this unit when it was renamed MOTU, retaining the code Y. It was withdrawn to No.23 Maintenance Unit on 9 June 1958 and placed in storage before being dismantled in October 1963. Colour scheme remained unchanged, comprising over overall Dark Sea Grey finish although white codes were later changed to red outlined in white, and red serials.

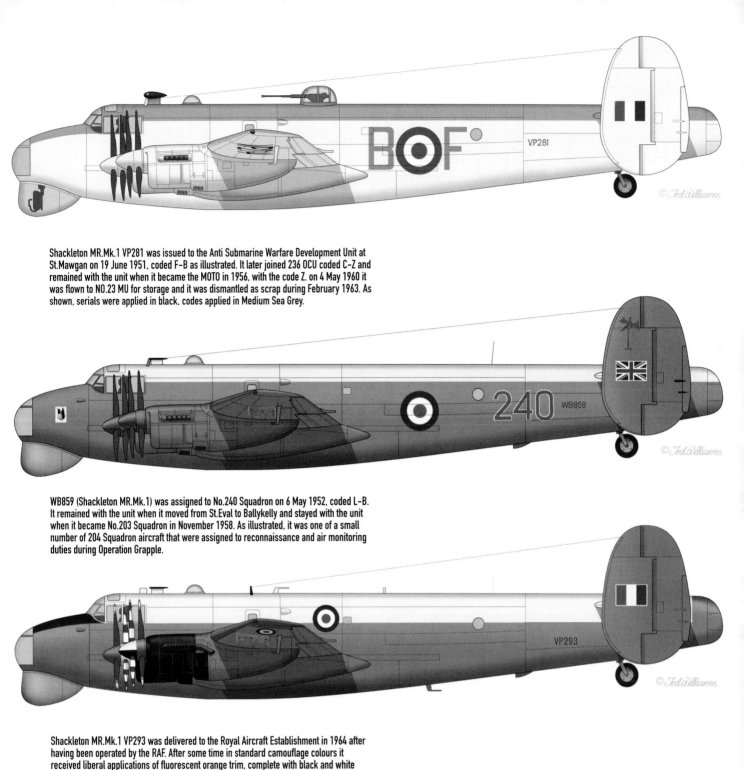

Shackleton MR.Mk.1 VP281 was issued to the Anti Submarine Warfare Development Unit at St.Mawgan on 19 June 1951, coded F-B as illustrated. It later joined 236 OCU coded C-Z and remained with the unit when it became the MOTO in 1956, with the code Z. on 4 May 1960 it was flown to NO.23 MU for storage and it was dismantled as scrap during February 1963. As shown, serials were applied in black, codes applied in Medium Sea Grey.

WB859 (Shackleton MR.Mk.1) was assigned to No.240 Squadron on 6 May 1952, coded L-B. It remained with the unit when it moved from St.Eval to Ballykelly and stayed with the unit when it became No.203 Squadron in November 1958. As illustrated, it was one of a small number of 204 Squadron aircraft that were assigned to reconnaissance and air monitoring duties during Operation Grapple.

Shackleton MR.Mk.1 VP293 was delivered to the Royal Aircraft Establishment in 1964 after having been operated by the RAF. After some time in standard camouflage colours it received liberal applications of fluorescent orange trim, complete with black and white spinners and propellers. The fluorescent orange was later changed to a more durable gloss bright orange. After being retired to the Strathallan Museum in Scotland it was subsequently broken-up and only the nose section now survives.

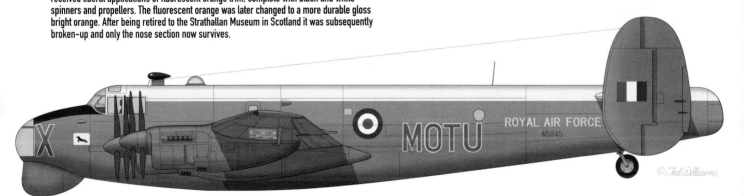

WB845 (Shackleton T.Mk.4) was manufactured as an MR.Mk.1 aircraft, issued to No.224 Squadron in February 1952, coded B-O. It then joined 236 OCU coded C-X and in October 1960 it was ferried to Langar for conversion to T.Mk.4 trainer standard. It then returned to the OCU (now named MOTU) and transferred to the MOTU's new home at St.Mawgan in July 1975 coded X as illustrated. It was withdrawn on 5 July 1968 and scrapped in 1969

Shackleton AEW.Mk.2 Sections

1. NOSE SECTION
2. FRONT CENTRE SECTION
3. INTERMEDIATE CENTRE SECTION
4. REAR CENTRE SECTION
5. REAR SECTION
6. TAIL PLANE
7. ELEVATOR
8. FIN
9. RUDDER
10. TAIL-WHEEL UNIT
11. INNER FLAP
12. CENTRE PLANE TRAILING EDGE
13. INBOARD REAR NACELLE FAIRING
14. INTERMEDIATE PLANE TRAILING EDGE
15. OUTBOARD FLAP
16. OUTBOARD FLAP EXTENSION
17. AILERON
18. WING TIP TRAILING EDGE
19. OUTER MAIN PLANE
20. INTERMEDIATE MAIN PLANE
21. OUTBOARD REAR NACELLE FAIRING
22. OUTBOARD ENGINE SUB-FRAME
23. OUTBOARD ENGINE FIREWALL
24. OUTBOARD POWER PLANT
25. MAIN LANDING GEAR DOOR
26. LANDING GEAR BAY VALANCE
27. MAIN LANDING GEAR
28. LANDING GEAR BEAM
29. INBOARD ENGINE SUB-FRAME
30. INBOARD ENGINE FIREWALL
31. INBOARD POWER PLANT
32. BOMB DOOR
33. RADAR BAY DOORS
34. RADOME

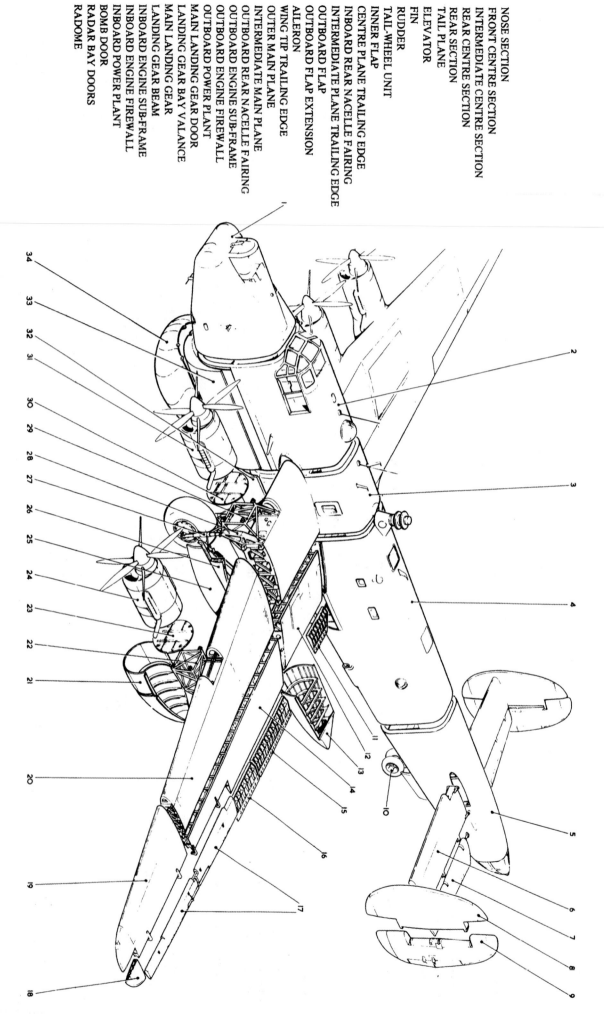

76

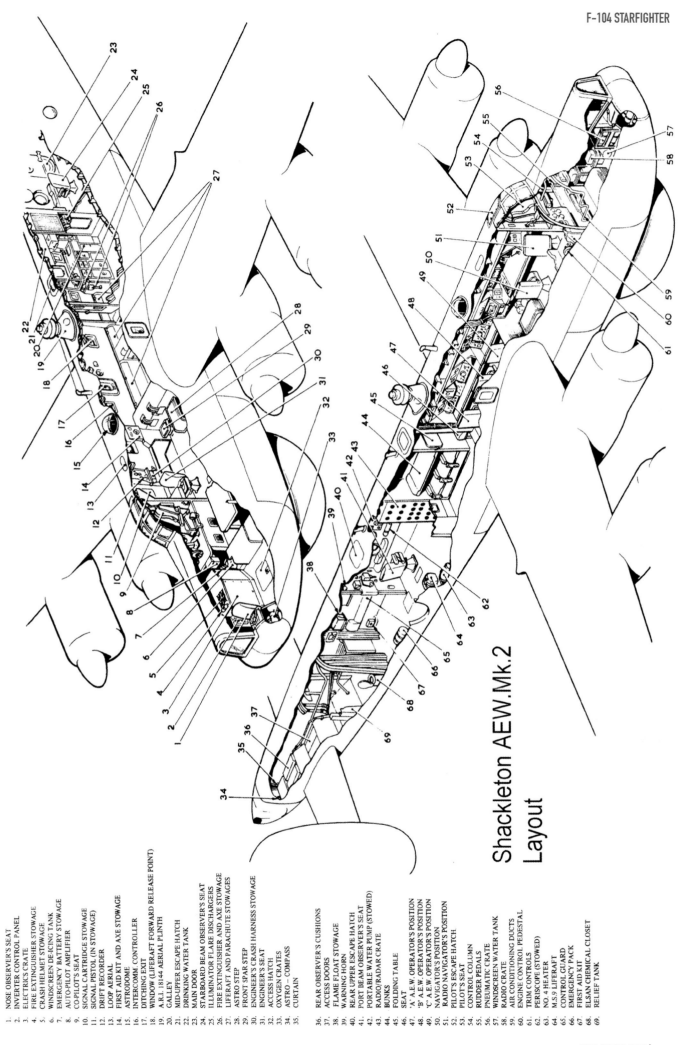

Shackleton AEW.Mk.2 Layout

1. NOSE OBSERVER'S SEAT
2. INVERTER CONTROL PANEL
3. ELECTRICS CRATE
4. FIRE EXTINGUISHER STOWAGE
5. CRASH HELMET STOWAGE
6. WINDSCREEN DE-ICING TANK
7. EMERGENCY BATTERY STOWAGE
8. AUTO-PILOT AMPLIFIER
9. CO-PILOT'S SEAT
10. SIGNAL CARTRIDGE STOWAGE
11. SIGNAL PISTOL (IN STOWAGE)
12. DRIFT RECORDER
13. LOOP AERIAL
14. FIRST AID KIT AND AXE STOWAGE
15. ASTRODOME
16. INTERCOMM. CONTROLLER
17. DITCHING EXIT
18. WINDOW (LIFERAFT FORWARD RELEASE POINT)
19. A.R.I. 18144 AERIAL PLINTH
20. GALLEY
21. MID-UPPER ESCAPE HATCH
22. DRINKING WATER TANK
23. MAIN DOOR
24. STARBOARD BEAM OBSERVER'S SEAT
25. ILLUMINATOR FLARE DISCHARGERS
26. FIRE EXTINGUISHER AND AXE STOWAGE
27. LIFERAFT AND PARACHUTE STOWAGES
28. ASTRO STEP
29. FRONT SPAR STEP
30. ENGINEER'S CRASH HARNESS STOWAGE
31. ENGINEER'S SEAT
32. ACCESS HATCH
33. OXYGEN CRATES
34. ASTRO – COMPASS
35. CURTAIN
36. REAR OBSERVER'S CUSHIONS
37. ACCESS DOORS
38. FLAME FLOAT STOWAGE
39. WARNING HORN
40. REAR UPPER ESCAPE HATCH
41. PORT BEAM OBSERVER'S SEAT
42. PORTABLE WATER PUMP (STOWED)
43. RADIO/RADAR CRATE
44. BUNKS
45. FOLDING TABLE
46. SEAT
47. 'A' A.E.W. OPERATOR'S POSITION
48. 'B' A.E.W. OPERATOR'S POSITION
49. 'C' A.E.W. OPERATOR'S POSITION
50. NAVIGATOR'S POSITION
51. RADIO NAVIGATOR'S POSITION
52. PILOT'S ESCAPE HATCH
53. PILOT'S SEAT
54. CONTROL COLUMN
55. RUDDER PEDALS
56. WINDSCREEN WATER TANK
57. PNEUMATIC CRATE
58. RADIO CRATE
59. AIR CONDITIONING DUCTS
60. ENGINE CONTROL PEDESTAL
61. TRIM CONTROLS
62. PERISCOPE (STOWED)
63. NO. 4 HEATER
64. M.S.9 LIFERAFT
65. CONTROL GUARD
66. EMERGENCY PACK
67. FIRST AID KIT
68. ELSAN CHEMICAL CLOSET
69. RELIEF TANK

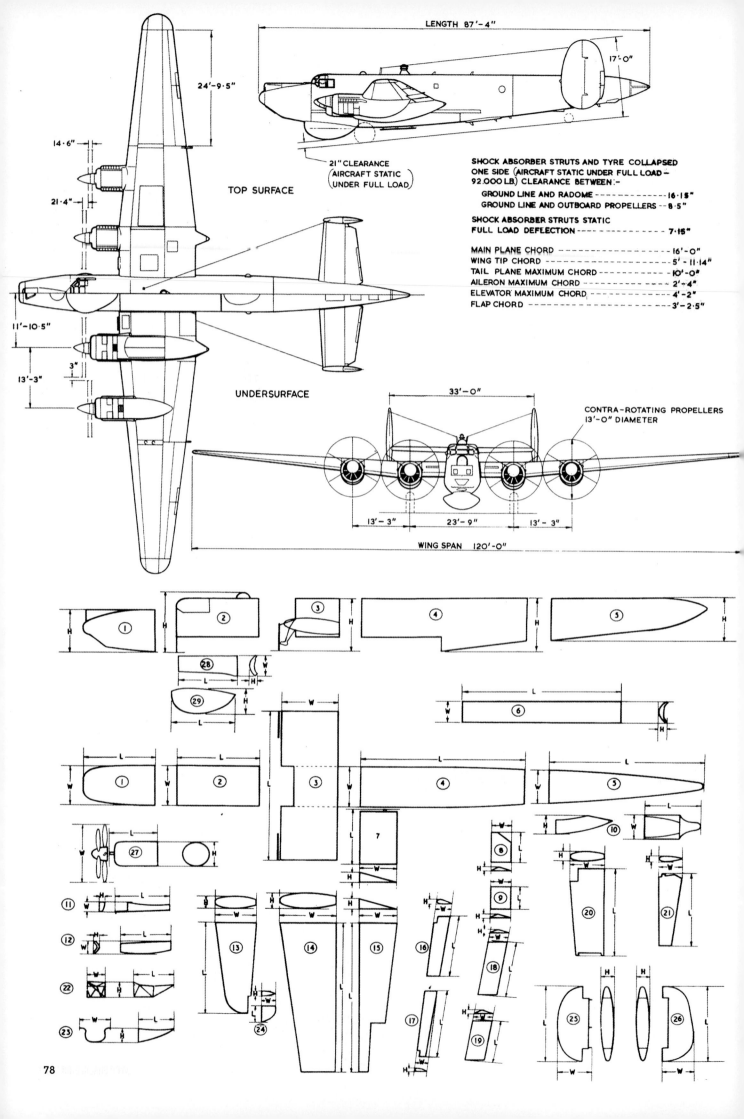

LENGTH 87'-4"

24'-9.5"

17'-0"

TOP SURFACE

21" CLEARANCE
(AIRCRAFT STATIC
UNDER FULL LOAD)

14·6"

21·4"

11'-10·5"

3"

13'-3"

UNDERSURFACE

SHOCK ABSORBER STRUTS AND TYRE COLLAPSED
ONE SIDE (AIRCRAFT STATIC UNDER FULL LOAD—
92,000 LB.) CLEARANCE BETWEEN:—
    GROUND LINE AND RADOME ----------- 16·15"
    GROUND LINE AND OUTBOARD PROPELLERS -- 8·5"

SHOCK ABSORBER STRUTS STATIC
FULL LOAD DEFLECTION ------------- 7·15"

MAIN PLANE CHORD ------------------ 16'-0"
WING TIP CHORD -------------------- 5'-11·14"
TAIL PLANE MAXIMUM CHORD ---------- 10'-0"
AILERON MAXIMUM CHORD ------------- 2'-4"
ELEVATOR MAXIMUM CHORD ------------ 4'-2"
FLAP CHORD ------------------------ 3'-2·5"

33'-0"

CONTRA-ROTATING PROPELLERS
13'-0" DIAMETER

13'-3"   23'-9"   13'-3"

WING SPAN   120'-0"

78

COMPONENT WEIGHTS AND DIMENSIONS

Item		Height (ft.)	Length (ft.)	Width (ft.)	Weight (lb.)
1	NOSE WITH EQUIPMENT	8.00	11.75	7.50	2 717
2	FRONT CENTRE SECTION WITH EQUIPMENT	11.66	13.50	8.00	5 235
3	INTERMEDIATE CENTRE SECTION WITH EQUIPMENT LESS LANDING GEAR	9.50	28.75	7.75	8 500
4	REAR CENTRE SECTION WITH EQUIPMENT	13.25	27.10	8.00	6 865
5	REAR SECTION WITH EQUIPMENT LESS LANDING GEAR	8.50	27.75	6.25	1 520
6	BOMB DOOR	1.33	22.67	5.00	286
7	CENTRE PLANE TRAILING EDGE	3.00	10.50	6.50	275
8	INNER FLAP	0.50	5.66	3.50	25
9	DUMMY FLAP	0.50	4.75	3.50	14
10	INBOARD REAR NACELLE FAIRING	3.50	10.50	4.75	50
11	VALANCE	0.50	9.75	2.00	16
12	MAIN-WHEEL UNIT DOOR	1.00	9.00	3.00	34
13	OUTER WING SECTION	1.50	17.00	7.50	400
14	INTERMEDIATE WING SECTION	3.00	29.00	9.75	2 600
15	INTERMEDIATE TRAILING EDGE	2.75	29.00	6.50	400
16	INBOARD AILERON SECTION	0.75	12.00	3.33	90
17	OUTBOARD AILERON SECTION	0.75	13.50	2.50	70
18	OUTER FLAP	0.50	12.33	3.50	52
19	OUTER FLAP EXTENSION	0.50	7.00	3.50	30
20	TAIL PLANE	1.50	17.00	7.50	349
21	ELEVATOR	0.75	13.25	4.00	170
22	OUTBOARD SUB-FRAME	3.50	8.00	3.25	207
23	OUTBOARD REAR NACELLE FAIRING	4.00	7.00	5.00	34
24	DETACHABLE WING TIP	0.50	3.25	2.50	11
25	FIN	1.00	14.50	6.00	165
26	RUDDER	1.00	14.50	5.25	173
27	POWER PLANT (INCLUDING PROPELLERS)	5.00	8.50	13.25	3 940
28	RADAR BAY DOOR	1.66	10.58	3.75	156
29	RADOME	4.08	11.75	8.60	244

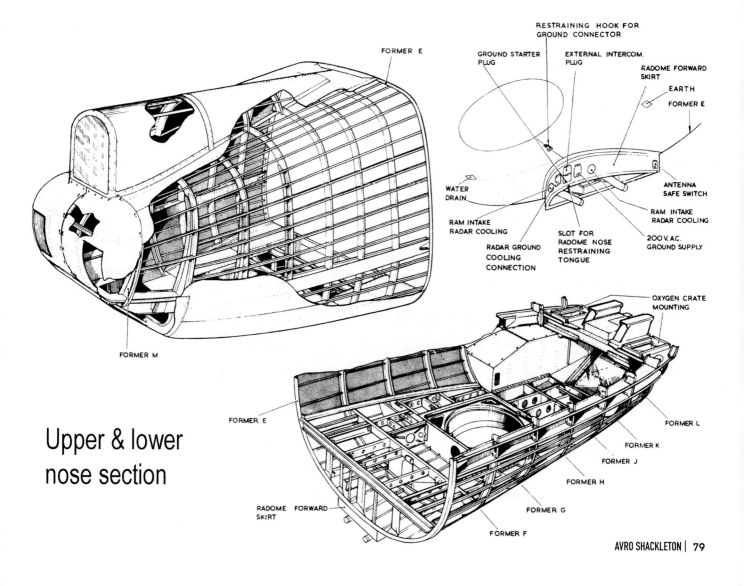

Upper & lower nose section

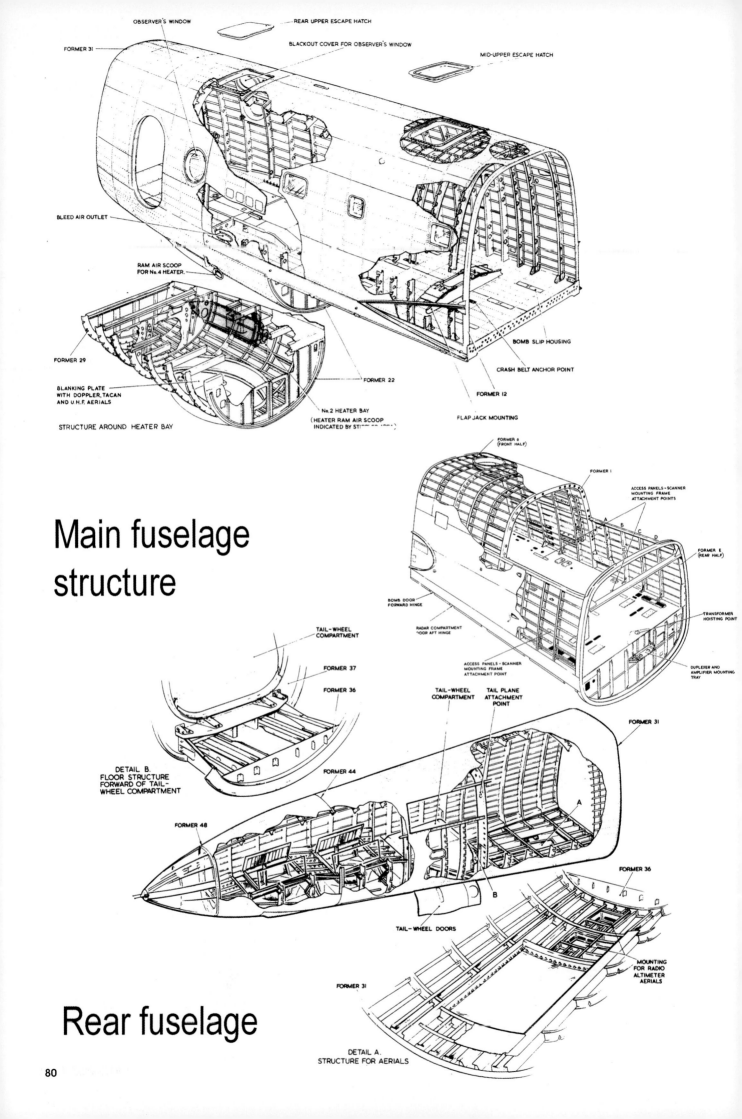

OBSERVER'S WINDOW

REAR UPPER ESCAPE HATCH

BLACKOUT COVER FOR OBSERVER'S WINDOW

MID-UPPER ESCAPE HATCH

FORMER 31

BLEED AIR OUTLET

RAM AIR SCOOP FOR No.4 HEATER.

FORMER 29

BLANKING PLATE WITH DOPPLER, TACAN AND U.H.F. AERIALS

STRUCTURE AROUND HEATER BAY

FORMER 22

No.2 HEATER BAY
(HEATER RAM AIR SCOOP INDICATED BY STIPPLE AREA)

BOMB SLIP HOUSING

CRASH BELT ANCHOR POINT

FORMER 12

FLAP JACK MOUNTING

Main fuselage structure

FORMER 6 (FRONT HALF)

FORMER 1

ACCESS PANELS - SCANNER MOUNTING FRAME ATTACHMENT POINTS

A B C D

FORMER E (REAR HALF)

TRANSFORMER HOISTING POINT

BOMB DOOR FORWARD HINGE

RADAR COMPARTMENT DOOR AFT HINGE

ACCESS PANELS - SCANNER MOUNTING FRAME ATTACHMENT POINT

DUPLEXER AND AMPLIFIER MOUNTING TRAY

TAIL-WHEEL COMPARTMENT

FORMER 37

FORMER 36

DETAIL B.
FLOOR STRUCTURE FORWARD OF TAIL-WHEEL COMPARTMENT

FORMER 44

TAIL-WHEEL COMPARTMENT

TAIL PLANE ATTACHMENT POINT

FORMER 31

FORMER 48

A

B

FORMER 36

TAIL-WHEEL DOORS

MOUNTING FOR RADIO ALTIMETER AERIALS

Rear fuselage

FORMER 31

DETAIL A.
STRUCTURE FOR AERIALS

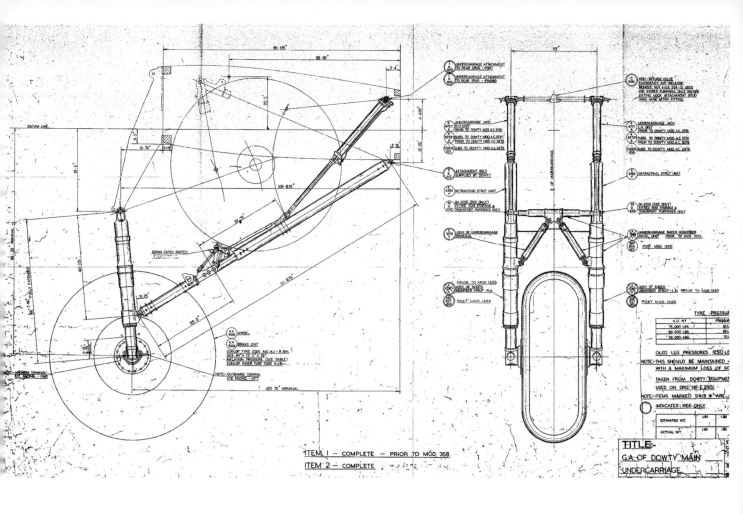

▲ Shackleton Mk.2
Main wheel assembly

▲ Shackleton MR.Mk.2
Tail wheel assembly

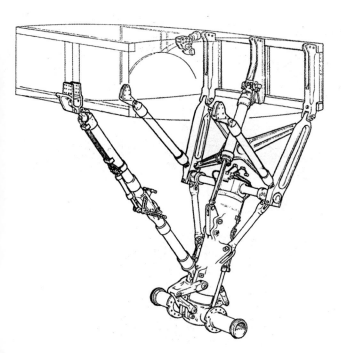

Shackleton MR.Mk.3
Main undercarriage unit

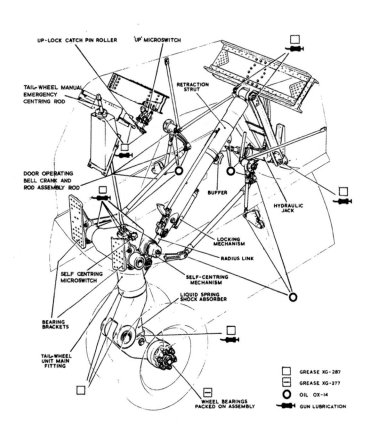

RETIREMENT AND RESURRECTION

The RAF's maritime reconnaissance fleet approaches retirement. But the Shackleton returns, ready for a new life in a very different role.

Presumably the No Parking sign didn't apply to Shackletons. A busy scene at RAF St.Mawgan during the 1960s, with resident 206 Squadron aircraft parked on the west pan, while a visiting Shackleton MR.Mk.2 from 224 Squadron taxies for take-off, on a long flight back to Gibraltar.
(Photo: Ashley Annis)

Following the loss of the Shackleton MR.Mk.3 prototype, the second aircraft assumed most of the type's evaluation and trials work. WR971 made its first flight on 28 May 1956 and remained in use with Avro and the A&AEE until 1960 when it was allocated to 120 Squadron during October coded E. It remained with Kinloss squadrons until withdrawal on 21 December 1970 when it was flown to Cosford for No.2SoTT. Used for ground instruction, it was sold in 1988 and dismantled, the nose section saved for preservation. *(Photo: Aeroplane)*

In line with modifications made to the Shackleton Mk.2 fleet, the MK.3 fleet was subjected to the same phased improvements, and aircraft from XF707 onwards were completed to Phase I standard with ASV Mk.21 radar, ILS, a VHF homer, a Mk.5 radio altimeter, auto pilot, Doppler and provision for "Orange Harvest" ECM equipment. Other changes included the deletion of the propeller de-icing system as this had consistently failed to work, and this was removed from the earlier Mk.3 aircraft when they were subsequently modified (by No.49 MU at Colerne). The last Mk.3 to be manufactured (and therefore the last Shackleton to be produced) was XF730, completed on 31 May 1959 and delivered a few days later to No.206 Squadron. By this stage work was commencing on a Phase II improvement programme, with WR972 acting as a trials aircraft. The Mk.3 fleet received Phase II modifications at either Langar or Colerne, following the same programme that had been applied to the Shackleton Mk.2. The aircraft emerged with little obvious external evidence of improvements, although the new ECM plinth situated on top of the fuselage indicated that Phase II modifications had been made. The programme was designed to enable Coastal Command's full strength to be maintained, with only a handful of aircraft being withdrawn for modification at any given time, and this meant that the Phase II wasn't completed until the end of 1963 when plans

The Mk.3 Shackleton's new tricycle undercarriage improved the aircraft's handling during take-off and landing, but the nose landing gear was prone to retraction failure and/or and collapse, as illustrated by this all-grey Shackleton from 220 Squadron making a rather unconventional landing at St.Mawgan.
(Photos: Tim McLelland collection)

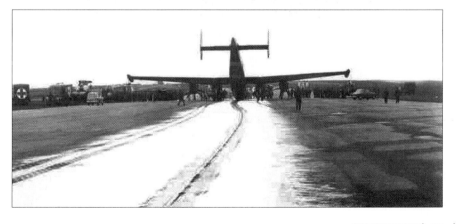

WR977 made its first flight on 31 August 1957, joining 220 Squadron in October of that year, coded L. It then moved to 201 Squadron and remained with this unit until modified to Phase III standard with Viper engines. It joined 42 Squadron and moved to Malta to join 203 Squadron in August 1970. It remained here until being withdrawn in November 1971 when it was allocated to Thorney Island for fire fighting use but a last minute change saw the aircraft go to Finningley on 8 November for preservation. It was transported to the Newark Air Museum by road on 1 May 1977 and remains on display there. *(Photo: Tim McLelland collection)*

XF711 is seen at St.Mawgan during 1966 whilst assigned to 42 Squadron. The squadron number is painted on the fuselage side in red (outlined in white) and serials are applied in red (outlined in white under the wings). The unit's bade is on the tail and a union flag is applied to the nose, indicating that the aircraft had been on an overseas visit. Also just visible are white "creep" markings on the nose wheel. XF711 was withdrawn in June 1971 and expired on Abingdon's fire dump during the early 1970s. *(Photo: Tim McLelland collection)*

WR984 is pictured whilst operating with 201 Squadron in 1963. Having flown for the first time on 6 March 1968, the aircraft had previously operated with 206 and 203 Squadrons. After modification to Phase III standard the aircraft joined 120 Squadron at Kinloss coded C and remained there until November 1967 when it returned to St.Mawgan. It was retired on 9 November 1970 and flown to Topcliffe for use as a ground instructional airframe 8115M. *(Photo: Tim McLelland collection)*

for Phase III were underway. As with the Shackleton Mk.2, the Phase III programme was rather more ambitious and three aircraft (WR974, WR982 and XF711) were allocated to trials. Major structural modifications were made, as well as major changes to the crew's Tactical station (resulting in a smaller galley area). In addition to new weapon options (most notably the MK.10 nuclear depth charge) and avionics improvements, the aircraft's Griffon engines were also modified to incorporate larger gearbox drives that were necessary to handle the greater electrical loads. This resulted in the engines be redesignated as the Griffon 58. The combined improvements raised the aircraft's weight still further, and in order to meet the aircraft's range requirements, it was proposed that the aircraft's all-up weight limit be raised to 105,000lb. Clearly, this would reduce the aircraft's marginal take-off performance still further, and this prompted another

examination of assisted take-off options. The concept of fitting a DH Spectre rocket motor under each wing was again considered, but eventually it was decided that the Bristol Siddeley Viper engine would be most suitable, housed in a redesigned outer engine nacelle fairing. WR973 (already undergoing modification to Phase III standard at Woodford) was duly modified, emerging for test flights with a pair of 2,500lb jet engines, on 29 February 1965. Placing the new engines in the aircraft's outer nacelles was a questionable decision, given the risks of asymmetric handling difficulties that might occur if one of the engines failed. But the turbojet was too large to simply be fixed to the rear of the inner nacelles (unlike a rocket pack that could be fixed externally), and Avro were obliged to create a new (but surprisingly elegant) outer nacelle fairing to position the Viper behind the Griffon's fire wall, with a ventral air intake covered by a retractable

door. Test flights with the engines were conducted from Boscombe Down and although they were successful, the engines could only be operated for a maximum of five minutes at full power. The reason for this was that the Viper required kerosene (Avtur) as fuel, but with Griffon engines, the Shackleton had a high-octane petrol (Avgas) system, and the Viper accumulated lead deposits on its turbine blades if operated for extensive periods on Avgas. The engine could operate at cruise setting for up to four hours, but it was take-off assistance that mattered most, and five minutes of full-power operation was more than enough. Vipers were introduced on all Mk.3 aircraft from May 166 onwards, with all squadrons operating fully modified Mk.3 aircraft by the end of 1968.

The Phase III aircraft fitted with Viper engines (it should be noted that the jet engine was not actually part of the upgrade programme) was in effect the ultimate

XF701 joined 120 Squadron in October 1958 but by May 1960 the aircraft had been withdrawn for Phase I modifications and use as a trials aircraft on cooling and cupola de-misting projects. It returns to RAF service in August 1962 coded E with 42 Squadron. In February 1965 it was transferred to 201 Squadron and modification to Phase III standard (with Vipers) was completed in April 1966. After a spell with 206 Squadron the aircraft joined the Kinloss Wing and moved south to 42 Squadron at St.Mawgan in June 1970 coded B and H. It was flown to the Central Training Establishment at Manston on 13 August 1971 and eventually destroyed after use for fire fighting training. *(Photo: Tim McLelland collection*

WR973 made its first flight on 18 January 1957 and was delivered to 203 Squadron in February 1960. By this stage the aircraft had spent years with Avro and HAS for various trials including vibration, ventilation and fuel system projects. It was modified to Phase III standard and used as a trials aircraft for the Viper installation before being delivered to 206 Squadron at Kinloss in May 1966 coded U. It moved to St. Mawgan in December 1970, joining 42 Squadron coded B. It was retired on 14 June 1971 and flown to Thorney Island for fire fighting training. *(Photo: Tim McLelland collection)*

206 Squadron Shackletons pictured at rest under grey skies at Kinloss. This squadron operated Shackletons from Kinloss from 1965 until 1970, the resident squadrons eventually being operated as part of a combined Wing arrangement. Squadron markings were mostly removed and all aircraft were finished in the standard Dark Sea Grey finish with white fuselage tops and red serials (outlined in red under the wing surfaces). *(Photo: Tim McLelland collection)*

expression of the Shackleton design, with stronger wing spars, re-skinned wings, slightly larger fuel tanks, greatly improved soundproofing for the crew, and other avionics improvements. But it was still a Shackleton, and in many respects it was the same aeroplane that had first appeared in 1949. Although performance and capability gradually improved, the Shackleton MR.Mk.3 Phase III boasted a range of 2,300nm – just 140 miles more than the original MR.Mk.1. It was nowhere near the kind of distance that the Air Ministry was aiming for, if it was to finally close the North Atlantic "gap" that had been such a thorny problem for the RAF throughout World War Two. The Shackleton had been a very significant improvement over the Lancasters that it directly replaced, but it had consistently failed to meet the performance figures that Coastal Command had hoped for, and had the RAF not been so eager to rapidly increase its MPA (Maritime

Patrol Aircraft) capability, the Shackleton might well have been abandoned after the first Mk.1 aircraft were delivered. But the demands on the MPA, force continued to increase as Soviet surface and sub-surface activity grew, eventually requiring Coastal Command to add five hours (ten percent) to each aircraft's monthly total by the summer of 1964, in order to meet the RAF's and Royal Navy's demands. Other aircraft could have been developed for the maritime role, but once the Shackleton was in service, the cheapest and swiftest replacement option was always another Shackleton.

By 1964 however, defence thinking was starting to change, and the Air Staff began to take a wider view of maritime capability. Instead of dwelling primarily on the performance of the aircraft, the changes in Soviet technology (particularly the advent of nuclear submarines that were almost impossible to detect or monitor) led to an

acceptance that more sophisticated reconnaissance and anti-submarine warfare techniques should be developed that were more suitable for the future. It was expected that the Mk.2 Shackleton would be unable to continue flying beyond 1970 although the later Shackleton MR.Mk.3 could continue flying until the late 1970s. This meant that an interim aircraft would be required to maintain squadron strength until the Shackleton Mk.3 was retired. Various options were considered for both the shorter-term and longer-term requirements, but acquiring yet another version of the Shackleton was never one of them. Derivatives of the BAC-111, Trident and VC10 were considered and although the Trident emerged as the preferred design, it was soon deemed to be far too expensive. By far the best option appeared to be the Breguet Atlantic, but France refused to accept British proposals for a significant amount of RAF Atlantic production to be moved to the

UK. There were hopes that a "quid pro quo" arrangement could be settled whereby France would purchase the British P.1154, but when this plan also failed, the British Government's interest shifted towards Hawker Siddeley's proposal for a maritime derivative of the Comet airliner, and during 1965 the HS.801 (Nimrod) was selected as the future replacement for the entire Shackleton fleet. There was soon no longer any need to look for an interim aircraft as it quickly became evident that the Viper engines were taking a heavy toll on the Shackleton Mk.3's fatigue life, and that they would be incapable of continuing in service for much longer than their older Mk.2 counterparts. Rather pointlessly, XF705 was fitted with a new airstream direction detector set combined with a pre-stall "stick shaker" during the early months of 1969, in an effort to finally equip the Mk.3 variant with an adequate warning system. The Mk.3 fleet was duly refitted with this system, even though all of the aircraft were just months away from withdrawal, as the new Nimrod neared completion. WR974 became the very last Shackleton to emerge from final refurbishment at the Hawker Siddeley Bitteswell facility (Langar having closed early in 1969) during March 1970, but after just eight months it was withdrawn and flown to Cosford for use as a ground instructional airframe. The last RAF Shackleton Mk.3 to remain in use was XF703, and this remained with No.42 Squadron at St.Mawgan until 23 September 1971, when it made one final flight to RAF Henlow. Incredibly, it was scrapped just three years later, the efforts to save this historical airframe (and land it on a very small grass landing strip) being ignored by the new RAF Museum, to whom the aircraft now belonged.

With the Shackleton Mk.3 gone, it was the MR.Mk.2 that soldiered on for a short time, although no longer as part of Coastal Command's MPA or ASW (Anti Submarine Warfare) force. Overseas commitments were still in place, including a detachment in Madagascar, from where reconnaissance patrols were flown by Shackleton crews in order to monitor the security of the Beira Straits (sanctions having been applied against Rhodesia through which the UN hoped to deny oil supplies to that country). Normally a couple of Shacketons were based at Majunga for this purpose, detached from No.204 Squadron at Ballykelly. When that station finally closed at the end of March 1971, the squadron was moved to Honington, from where the detachment continued to be supported, the rest of the unit being assigned to Search and Rescue duties (although other overseas detachments were also still in place). Operations continued until the Madagascar detachment was ended on 17 March 1972, and the squadron finally stood-down on 28 April, marking the very end of RAF Shackleton

WR983 is pictured out over the Atlantic whilst assigned to 206 Squadron in 1963. This photograph illustrates the excellent visibility afforded to the pilots, thanks to the Mk.3's redesigned canopy structure. Also clearly visible is the plinth for the "Orange Harvest" Electronic Counter Measures sensor (a radar warning receiver), which has been removed for servicing. *(Photo: Aeroplane)*

operations – or so it seemed at that time. Back in 1965 the Government had abandoned all future aircraft carrier developments, and this move meant that as the existing carrier fleet slowly wound-down, the Royal Navy and RAF would no longer have any form of airborne early warning platform. AEW had become an increasingly important asset, but after being deprived of its ambitious carrier programme, the possibility of using converted helicopters as AEW aircraft was – almost petulantly -refused by the Navy. The RAF had already begun looking for a potential AEW aircraft in order to improve its defence radar network, and with the prospect of the Navy's AEW Gannets being withdrawn when HMS Ark Royal was retired, the responsibility of providing radar cover for naval forces in the Atlantic would shift to the RAF. Hawker Siddeley Aviation proposed a version of its HS.801 but it was judged to be unnecessarily large and complex, and a derivative of the

Andover transport was considered in more detail, until it too was dropped on the basis that it was rapidly becoming a completely new machine rather than a mere conversion of existing surplus airframes. Instead, the Boeing E-3 AWACS (Airborne Warning And Control System) was chosen, despite the obvious fact that it was even more sophisticated than the HS.801 project that had been offered by Hawker Siddeley. But with the prospect of joint procurement with European allies, and projected commonality with USAF forces, it looked like an attractive idea, but seemingly endless prevarication during the procurement arrangements indicated that by the time that the E-3 was ready for delivery, Britain would have had no AEW aircraft for some time and existing radar interpretation expertise would have been lost, at the very time when the need for AEW cover was becoming more important than ever. The only practical solution was to look allow history to

repeat itself yet again, and look at another version of the Shackleton, configured to carry the radar equipment taken from the Navy's retired Gannets.

This "austere" solution was intended to me only a temporary measure to maintain AEW capability until American E-3 aircraft could be acquired. The radar equipment was old (originally carried in AEW Skyraiders before the Gannets) but it was reliable, and despite the Shackleton's many shortcomings, it was easily capable of carrying the radar and its displays, with plenty of room for crew. Most importantly, numerous examples of the Shackleton were readily available, with many still in service. The Shackleton Mk.3 seemed like the logical candidate for conversion to the AEW role, but the Mk.3 aircraft had been flown extensively, and with their heavy Viper jets contributing to fatigue, they were unsuitable for further use. Conversely, the older Mk.2 aircraft were lighter, did not have Viper jets,

and had recently been re-sparred after fatigue life had again become a critical issue. The proposal was accepted and WL745 was withdrawn from No.204 Squadron during March 1970 and flown to Woodford, where cruise performance testing was conducted and the new engineering issues were examined. Conversion of WL745 to AEW standard began five months later, the ASV Mk.21 radar being removed and a new (or to be more precise, old) AN/APS 20 equipment was installed in an external fairing under the forward bomb bay, the bomb bay doors being reduced in length to close behind the radar fairing. Inside the fuselage the Tactical station was redesigned to accommodate a new crew

layout, but in overall terms the aircraft remained largely unchanged, and even retained its white-topped maritime paint finish. Making its first flight as a Shackleton AEW.Mk.2 on 30 September 1971, it was flown to Boscombe Down for evaluation and acceptance trials during April 1972. A further 11 Mk.2 aircraft were selected for conversion, and these were dispatched to Bitteswell, beginning with WL747 on 2 February 1971. The full conversion process took some time and it wasn't until January 1972 that the aircraft left Bitteswell (via Kemble where it was repainted) for Lossiemouth, where it was fitted with radar equipment taken from a Gannet. No.8 Squadron reformed at Kinloss on 1

January 1972, initially equipped with a pair of standard Shackleton MR.Mk.2 (Phase III) aircraft, but on 11 April WL 747 arrived, followed by further aircraft over the following weeks. By the time that the unit had relocated to nearby Lossiemouth in August 1973, only WL745 was yet to be delivered, and this aircraft returned to Bitteswell for modifications after completing trials at Boscombe Down, joining No.8 Squadron in September after being brought up to a common standard.

The "new" AEW Shackletons were of course quite elderly machines, equipped with even more elderly radar, although the AN/APS 20F(I) equipment was improved thanks to the incorporation of Decca Doppler 72M which

South Africa's requirement for a new maritime aircraft to replace its Sunderland flying boats emerged in 1952 and an order for eight Shackletons was placed at the end of 1953, although the UK's Secretary of Commerce opposed the necessary import license, delaying a formal contract until March 1954. Essentially similar to the RAF's MK.3, the SAAF aircraft had a greater degree of soundproofing and improved crew facilities. They also retained the capability to carry lifeboats in view of the vast areas of sea that would be patrolled, and the relative scarcity of shipping. The first SAAF Shackleton (1716) made its first flight on 29 March 1957 and this, together with two more aircraft (1716 and 1717) were officially handed-over at a ceremony held at Woodford on 24 April. Five days later the aircraft were flown to St.Mawgan where the SAAF crews operated in co-operation with RAF Shackleton crews on training exercises. Despite issues with skin cracking that were rectified on site at St.Mawgan by an Avro team, the aircraft were flown to South Africa on 18 August, thereby enabling the SAAF to introduce the Mk.3 Shackleton into service some 12 days before the RAF. *(Photos: Aeroplane)*

provided good ground stabilization. Oragne Harvest ECM was also provided together with an APX7 IFF interrogator (active and passive). Communications equipment was also improved, and the complete package was found to be more than adequate as a short-term AEW solution. In overall terms the aircraft were largely unchanged from their previous maritime configurations, although the interior of the fuselage was slightly different with three radar control positions situated along the port side of the fuselage, aft of the main wing spar. The ageing radar was less-than perfect but former Gannet personnel from the Navy were assigned to the squadron to enable new RAF crews to learn

interpretation techniques from these veterans who knew better than anybody how to get the best from the equipment. Their task was soon made slightly easier after the incorporation of a Marconi-Elliott airborne moving-target indicator system, which filtered-out radar returns from surface vessels, thereby making it easier to detect airborne targets. By September 1972 the squadron was ready to be declared operational and over the following years the squadron gradually shifted its main responsibility from the provision of low-level air defence for naval forces, to wider air defence of the United Kingdom, operating in co-operation with No.11 Group's fighter assets. But despite being tasked with a role

that was very different to the one for which the Shackleton was designed, it was hardly surprising that the squadron's aircraft were still equipped with rescue gear so that they could provide Search and Rescue support if required.

Plans to provide the RAF with a completely new AEW platform continued, but progress was painfully slow, and by 1976 a final decision had still not been made, but by this stage the Shackletons were approaching the end of their wing spar fatigue lives again, and with no other practical option being available, it was agreed that the Shackletons should be modified yet again on a six-month rotational basis so that No.8 Squadron could maintain its

The remainder of the SAAF Shackleton fleet was delivered in February 1958. Aircraft 1723 suffered hydraulic failure and made a landing without brakes, swerving off the runway to avoid the perimeter road, all in front of assembled media. The aircraft settled into service, eventually receiving Phase I modification kits from Avro, despite steadily deteriorating relations between South African and British governments. A Hawker Siddeley team upgraded the aircraft to Phase II standard on site at Ysterplaat, where the SAAF's No.35 Squadron was based. Eventually the aircraft were modernized further, almost to an equivalent standard to the RAF's Phase III machines. Aircraft 1718 was lost on 8 August 1963 when it struck high ground in the Steynskloof Mountains in bad weather. The remaining aircraft were all to be re-sparred but only two examples were modified, as obtaining components for the aircraft became increasingly difficult, and in November 1977 aircraft 1723 was retired after reaching its fatigue limit. 1719 followed on 24 April 1978 and on 24 November 1984 the remainder of the Shackleton fleet was withdrawn. Two aircraft were retained for ceremonial display purposes, and one machine is still with the SAAF in airworthy condition, although it is currently grounded due to spares shortages and crew qualification issues.
(Photos: Aeroplane & Tim Mclelland collection)

operational strength. The first aircraft to be refurbished was WR963 and this aircraft flew to Bitteswell on 1 March 1976, to be followed by WR965 in September. Each aircraft remained at Bitteswell for approximately 12 months before returning to Lossiemouth to resume operational activity. It was expected that the aircraft would now continue to remain in service until a replacement aircraft was delivered, and in 1977 the Nimrod AEW. Mk.3 was selected as the RAF's new radar platform, using a batch of aircraft taken from the current maritime fleet. But although the Nimrod had already proven itself as a remarkably effective and reliable replacement for the Shackleton, the new radar equipment

being designed for it was completely new, and unproven. Meanwhile, the Government opted to halve the Shackleton fleet during 1981 as an economy measure. Given the limited number of available aircraft it was perhaps a token gesture towards economic prudence, but with the prospect of new Nimrods only two years away, it was probably inevitable that the Shackletons would be regarded as less important than they once were. The remaining support of naval operations ended and the aircraft were now almost exclusively assigned to the air defence of the north-eastern region of Britain's and Nato's air space, although the squadron still regularly participated in various exercises, venturing to locations such as

Iceland, Cyprus and mainland Europe. Meanwhile, the Nimrod programme continued but by the end of 1983 there was still no realistic prospect of the new AEW aircraft being delivered, thanks to endless delays in the aircraft's radar and systems development programmes. By 1985 the Shackletons were again in need of extensive modifications and repairs but with HAS's Bitteswell facility having closed, the MoD was obliged to look for a new means of refurbishing the remaining six aircraft on site at Lossiemouth, and various civilian contractors were invited to make a bid for the task. Airwork Services were awarded a contract and yet another modification

Pictured over the Cornish countryside, a Shackleton poses for the camera during a sortie from RAF St.Mawgan. This MR.Mk.3 is modified to Phae I standard and has yet to receive Orange Harvest ECM equipment and Viper turbojet boosers. *(Photo: Aeroplane)*

A stunning close–up look at a Shackleton MR.Mk.3 as it roars away from RAF Luqa's runway in Malta. The nose position is occupied by an observer and both he and the pilot are wearing crash helmets, although many crews often chose to dispense with these safety items. Clearly visible is the Griffon engine's exhaust pile, suppressing sound and directing its sooty exhaust trail downwards under the aircraft. *(Photo: Godfrey Mangion)*

No.203 Squadron's WR974 is pictured on final approach to RAF Luqa after completing a sortie over the Mediterranean. The Viper engine inlet doors can be seen in their extended position, indicating that both engines are running, in anticipation of a possible roller landing or overshoot on Luqa's relatively short (by Shackleton Mk.3 standards) runway. *(Photo: Godfrey Mangion)*

programme began in April 1986 (WL756 having already been subject to a trial modification programme during this process) with the last aircraft being completed in February 1988. By this stage the troubled Nimrod programme had finally been cancelled and an order for Boeing E-3 aircraft had been placed during the previous February, with the promise of new aircraft reaching the RAF in 1990. The Shackletons were therefore required to soldier-on, and it wasn't until March 1991 that the first E-3D was delivered to the RAF. On

1 July 1991 No.8 squadron officially reformed on the Sentry AEW.Mk.1 at Waddington and the AEW Shackletons were finally retired. Their 19 years of operational service had been quite an achievement for an aircraft that had been brought into service as a short-term "stop gap".

1991 was therefore the end of the Shackleton's uneventful but remarkably long operational life and with the last examples having been flown to their final destinations, the story of the Shackleton – and therefore

the entire story of the Lancaster family – was at almost at an end. Just two Shackletons remained airworthy in South Africa, having been retained for occasional display purposes following the type's retirement from SAAF service in 1984. One of these (1716) was to have returned to the UK during 1994, to appear at various air shows during the summer show season. Tragically, the flight to the UK ended in disaster following the failure of both starboard engines over the Sahara desert. The aircraft was crash landed

A classic photograph of the Shackleton MR.Mk.3, low down over the Atlantic in its operational environment. This Phase II aircraft carried Orange Harvest ECM and illustrates the white–painter propeller spinners, adopted by 120 Squadron. *(Photo: Aeroplane)*

No.42 Squadron's WR984 is pictured at RAF St.Mawgan early in 1968, after having been fitted with Viper engines late in 1966. It remained active until 9 November 1970 when it was ferried to Topcliffe, where it was allocated serial 8115M. *(Photo: Tim McLelland collection)*

XF703 is pictures at St.Mawgan in front of the Newquay Airport terminal, preparing for it's final flight on 23 September 1971 to HEnlow, where it was to be preserved by the RAF Museum as the last Shackleton Mk.3 in service with NO.18 group Strike Command. Tragically, the aircraft was dismantled some years later and was never placed on public display. *(Photo: Ashley Annis)*

and although the crew escape unhurt (and were subsequently rescued) the aircraft was written-off and abandoned. This left only 1722 in the SAAF's care and after being restored to full flight status, it continued to fly in South Africa for some time until rising operating costs and crew currency eventually forced the aircraft to be grounded again. It is unclear whether the aircraft will fly again although it is maintained in airworthy condition, therefore it may well re-appear if a new crew can be trained and qualified to fly

it, and sufficient funds (and spares) can be sourced. Back in the UK, the Shackleton Preservation Trust (formed by David Liddell-Grainger) purchased two former 8 Squadron Shackleton AEW2 aircraft (WL790 and WR963) and plans were made to fly WL790 as a civilian "warbird" with WR963 possibly acting as a spares source. After spending some time at Coventry Airport, efforts to gain CAA certification failed and the aircraft were transferred to the care of Air Atlantique. WL790 eventually departed for

the USA where FAA regulations permitted the aircraft to be flown (Britain's CAA having a far more demanding set of regulations that make the operation of such types almost impossible). Operated in Minnesota by Amjet, the aircraft made a few flights during its stay, while Air Atlantique continued to make efforts to gain CAA approval to operate the aircraft back in the UK. Sadly, no such agreement was reached and after a short stay with the Commemorative Air Force in Texas, the aircraft was finally flown to the Pima Air

WL745 pictured at Woodford in 1971 after conversion into Airborne Early Warning configuration. The new radar housing is clearly visible under the aircraft's forward fuselage, attached to the aircraft's bomb bay, with the bomb bay doors reduced in length to open behind the radar housing. Also visible is the test instrumentation boom attached to the aircraft's nose. It first flew in this configuration on 30 September 1971.
(Photo: Aeroplane)

This publicity photograph was taken shortly after WL745 began flying as the AEW trials installation aircraft. At this stage the aircraft still retained its paint scheme from previous service with 204 Squadron at Ballykelly, complete with white-toppe fuselage.
(Photo: Tim McLelland collection)

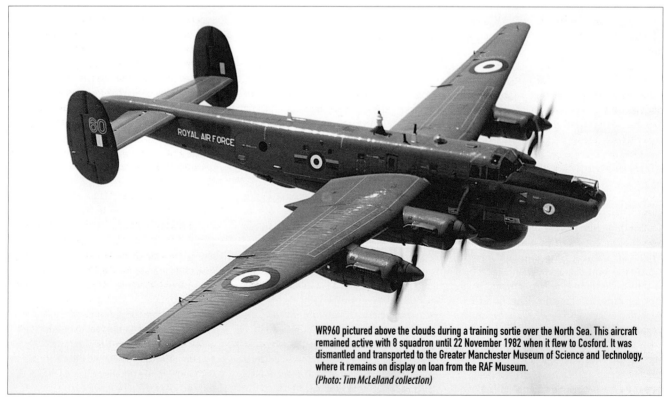

WR960 pictured above the clouds during a training sortie over the North Sea. This aircraft remained active with 8 squadron until 22 November 1982 when it flew to Cosford. It was dismantled and transported to the Greater Manchester Museum of Science and Technology, where it remains on display on loan from the RAF Museum.
(Photo: Tim McLelland collection)

WL747 made its first flight in AEW configuration on 11 January 1972 before joining 8 Squadron at Kinloss on 16 March of that year. It was retired from service at the end of June 1991 and flown to Paphos in Cyprus, having been sold to a civilian buyer. Sadly, plans to preserve and possibly fly the aircraft failed to materialize and the aircraft was abandoned on site. It remains there in derelict condition together with WL757 – the RAF's last operational Shackleton. *(Photo: Tim Mclelland collection)*

WL757 completed what was the last Shackleton flight in RAF service on 17 April 1991 before heading to Paphos in Cyrpus, where the aircraft was to have been preserved. Sadly, the plans were dropped and the aircraft was left abandoned. WR963 enjoyed a much happier retirement, and is now in the care of the Shackleton Preservation Trust at Coventry, hopefully to fly again in the future. Both aircraft sport red noses in support of a BBC charity event. *(Photo: Aeroplane)*

and Space Museum on 16 December 2007, where it is now placed on permanent static display. But back at Coventry, a group of volunteers had been restoring WR963 to static display condition, slowly replacing some of the aircraft's internal equipment with original MR.Mk.2 equivalents, while the AEW radome was removed and the aircraft repainted in "vintage" white and grey maritime colours. Eventually the Shackleton Preservation Trust was reformed and in 2012 a plan was devised to restore WR963 to flying condition, after negotiations with the CAA eventually indicated that the aircraft could be certified to fly, if necessary refurbishments were made. Now registered as G-SKTN, the aircraft is in fully functional condition and regular engine and taxy runs are made, much to the delight of many enthralled spectators. Plans to restore the aircraft to flying condition depend on the condition of the aircraft's wing spars, and when investigations into the costs of completing necessary work on this structure are completed, a fund-raising programme will go into full swing and hopefully WR963 will eventually return to the

skies again, more than 60 years after her first flight back in March 1954.

Avro's Shackleton could hardly be described as an outstanding design. It was in effect merely a development of an existing aircraft, and one that can be traced back to the troubled Manchester Bomber. It failed to meet many of the performance figures that were expected of it. It was brutally noisy, often cold and uncomfortable for its crews, with modest speed, cumbersome manoeuvrability, and many handling and maintenance issues that had to be grudgingly accepted as part of routine operations. But despite all these failings, the Shackleton was a remarkably successful aeroplane, and one that was admired and loved by air and ground crews alike. It was incredibly robust and it was reliable. It boasted a capacious fuselage interior that could accommodate whatever the RAF needed to put inside it, and it had an equally capacious bomb bay in which a huge variety of stores could be carried, ranging from rescue dinghies through to nuclear depth charges. But perhaps most importantly, the

Shackleton had the ability to endure. When it was seemingly nearing the end of its useful life it was simply rebuilt and returned into service, and this process of ongoing renewal enabled the aircraft to achieve an operational life span of remarkable proportions when compared to contemporary aircraft that often enjoyed useful lives that lasted maybe less than half as long. The Shackleton's monotonous maritime tasks were never likely to capture newspaper headlines, and it is no surprise that when compared to the glamorous fighters and fearsome bombers from the same era, the Shackleton rarely merits much attention. But there can be no doubt that the Shackleton was a hugely successful aeroplane. It was also a fascinating one, representing the very end of Avro's linear development of heavy bomber aircraft and the end of the RAF's association with the mighty four-engine bomber design. In many respects the mighty Shackleton marked the end of an era and although the roar of the Shackleton's Griffon engines may be long gone, the Shackleton's place in history is undoubtedly secured. ❖

Shackleton WR963 pictured at Leuchars whilst serving with No.8 Squadron as an AEW.Mk.2. It is currently with the Shackleton Preservation Trust at Coventry awaiting restoration to airworthy status. *(Photo: Ashley Annis)*

Long before reaching retirement and transportation to its final resting place in the Greater Manchester Museum of Science and Industry, WR960 flew a photo rendezvous sortie with a pre-production Nimrod AEW.Mk.3, illustrating what was to have been the handover of the RAF's AEW responsibilities from the Shackleton to the Nimrod. Within weeks of this image being captured the Nimrod programme was cancelled, and the Shackletons soldiered-on until the first deliveries of Boeing E-3D Sentries were made in 1991. *(Photo: Tim McLelland collection)*

AIRBORNE IN THE SHACKLETON

John Botwood describes a typical Shackleton training sortie from RAF Ballykelly, during the 1950s.

A sunny scene at St.Mawgan as 206 Squadron's XF707 taxies from the south pan for take-off. This photograph was taken before the huge new servicing hangar was built on the site of the hangar visible to the right of the picture. *(Photo: RAF Air Historical Branch)*

Being part of a Shackleton crew was always an interesting experience, particularly back in the 1950s and none of them was more interesting than the last month of one year. The chart in the A Flight Commander's office became the object of everyone's attention around mid-November in 1957. There was a green line starting at January and going directly to December with the squadron's allocated flying hours as the target. The red line that wobbled around the green, showed the progress of the squadron's actual flying hours, day by day. When it became obvious at the end of the year that the hours flown would not balance the Squadron's allocated hours, there was either nothing to do or there was a mad rush to accumulate as many hours as possible before Christmas. During the previous year the hours flown had outstripped the hours required and consequently the crews had hung around the crew room trying to find ways of passing the time. I was based at Ballykelly at that time and winter in Northern Ireland does not lend itself to many outdoor activities. November 1957 was typical of the latter case. Number 269 Squadron at Ballykelly had a red line that was short by 650 hours. So eight crews had to accumulate that amount in three to four weeks. To put it simply, we had to make each sortie a fifteen hour Navex, or Navigation Exercise.

There were three Coastal Command Squadrons at Ballykelly, all equipped with Avro Shackletons. Numbers 269 and 240 flew the Mk.1 and 204 flew the later Mk.2. Although different in appearance the two Marks had the same internal equipment. Each Squadron had nine aircraft, and their personnel were split into two Flights. There was A Flight with nine crews, each crew comprising two pilots, two navigators, one flight engineer and five signallers. Then there was B Flight that consisted of all the ground crew specialists necessary for maintaining the front line operation of the Squadron. Our main area of operations was the North Atlantic - sometimes called "The Pond" by us. You could say that it is an intriguing part of the world. It holds so much history, both apparent and hidden. Rockall for example, is a solitary landmark four hundred miles Northwest of Ireland, and is a small rocky pinnacle sometimes sixty feet above sea level, whereas at other times it is completely submerged. The Royal Navy claimed it for the United Kingdom in 1952 by landing a crewman from a Sikorsky Dragonfly to plant a flag. This was done on one of the Atlantic's quieter days, but the flagstaff was still there in 1962 (we saw it). Within thirty miles of the lonely rock lie four U-boat aces and many of their victims. Both hunter and hunted lie together there forever. Trans Atlantic air traffic was on the increase in 1957. The airline fleets consisted mainly of Super Constellations, Stratocruisers and DC-7s. The

Accompanying the previous image, another view of XF707, pictured as the pilot conducts his walk-round inspection of the aircraft. This photo clearly illustrates the nose-mounted guns and the small blister in the starboard side of the air gunner's canopy. *(Photo: Aeroplane collection)*

Ground crew attend to a 206 Squadron Shackleton MK.3's Rolls-Royce Griffon engine, during a visit to RAF Gibraltar. Given the size of the aircraft and the many deployments made by Shackleton units around the world, it was inevitable that most maintenance was conducted outdoors. *(Photo: Aeroplane collection)*

Comet and the Boeing 707 had commenced operations in September and October respectively and would soon change the scene. An average of 182 aircraft crossed in Mid Atlantic at 0200, usually some 20,000ft above us. We could listen to their chatter on VHF, whilst on the HF band the strange sounding chords of the four harmonic tones of the SELCAL (a selective calling radio system) could be heard. We did not have the required decoder, but we received the four harmonic tones loud and clear. Many calls were to the Ocean Weather Stations. These ships were no stranger to the North Atlantic, having served their time protecting convoys and hunting U-Boats some 12 years earlier.

They were converted corvettes and provided weather reporting to Europe and the British Isles. They could also provide direction finding, flare paths and Ground Controlled Approaches for us in an emergency. We would often exercise with them and conduct simulated ditching emergencies to keep their Ground Controlled Approach operators proficient in their talk-down procedures. We often operated with them in our Search and Rescue role and looked forward each year to dropping Christmas mail and tree to our 'local' Station Ocean Weather Station Juliett.

A typical Navex would be from 0600 to 2100 or 1800 to 0900. The 0600 flight started with an early morning call at 0300. Preflight

meals would be taken in the Messes and of course these would normally consist of bacon, eggs, sausages and beans. Then via either coach or van we would go to the Operations building at 0430 where each specialist would self brief before gathering in the main operations room for a general briefing. The pilots would come out of the Notice to Airmen and Mariners (Notam) office, while the signallers would finish discussions with the Ground Radio Operators in the adjoining room and collect the codes of the day. The navigators would have been checking the wall board and daily charts to see if our paths would cross with any other operations. A typical briefing would have the

Shackleton MR.Mk.3 XF708 was delivered to 201 Squadron already modified to Phase I standard (as illustrated) in March 1959, and after further modification to Phase II standard it was transferred to 120 Squadron coded A. It was then returned to HAS for Phase III improvements including installation of Viper engines, and after a period of trials work, it was delivered to 203 Squadron coded C in February 1967. It moved with the unit to Luqa in January 1969 and stayed there until January 1972 when it was placed in storage at Kemble. It was ferried to Duxford on 23 August 1972 for the Imperial War Museum and the aircraft remains on display at Duxford.
(Photo: Aeroplane)

Met Officer, followed by the Operations Officer giving an update on the intelligence situation on Nato and other forces in the Atlantic. Most days we would have the Pond to ourselves. If there was to be a depth charge drop, the promulgated area would be the subject of a Notam and it was not surprising to find the occasional trawler hanging about in the site. Sorties could be easily planned on a triangular course, each leg lasting four hours with crew training being carried out on an opportunity basis. Cruising altitudes would vary between 500 and 1,500ft depending on weather conditions. Fifteen hours and back home, this had to be the only RAF Command where an

aircraft left point A and after so long a time looking at nothing but sea, only to arrive back at point A! While the briefing was in progress, the ground crew would have been working on the aircraft for some hours. A fifteen hour flight required 3,626 gallons of Avgas, so with no fuel jettison system and a maximum take-off weight close to 81,000lbs this meant that once airborne, six to seven hours were required to burn off sufficient fuel to get down to landing weight again. The armourers would be loading the weapons bay which had fifteen stations, each capable of carrying l,000lbs except the centre station which could carry a 4,000lb airborne droppable lifeboat if necessary. A normal

training load would be 32 practice bombs (dropped in sticks of two, to mark the start and finish of a depth charge stick of six), six sonobuoys and four depth charges. The bombing practice was for pilots and navigators. Pilots dropped the depth charges from low level by eye and navigators dropped from 300ft using the bombsight. Practice runs could commence from any range and in the navigator's case were usually the result of a radar homing from eight miles. Sonobuoys were carried for investigation purposes and the depth charges as part of the annual allotment for proficiency training. You could see the results of a depth charge drop, which is more than

Shackleton MR.Mk.3 WR972 was undoubtedly the most unusual example of this variant. First flown on 6 November 1956, the aircraft was destined never to reach RAF service, and was retained for trails work with Avro and the A&AEE until April 1961 when it was transferred to the Royal Aircraft Establishment at Farnborough. It was assigned to testing of brake parachutes for the TSR2 programme for some time, and eventually assigned to other projects, most notably parachute drop trials of both personnel and equipment. For these roles the aircraft had the tail glazing removed and replaced by a specially-manufactured clear fairing from which parachute trials could be observed. This fairing could be removed if necessary and parachute attachment points could be fixed here. An attachment point and strain gauge was also fitted under the tail. The standard RAF grey and white paint scheme was soon modified to incorporate fluorescent orange patches on the nose, tail and wings, and after a few years of activity at Farnborough the grey and white finish was resprayed silver, with the orange patches still retained. The undersides of the aircraft were painted with black and yellow stripes although the aircraft was never used for target towing (for which these markings were normally applied). *(Photos: Tim Mclelland collection & Paul Platt)*

could be said for the annual drop of a homing torpedo which would enter the water with a splash and spend the rest of the time out of view, banging repeatedly against a "padded" submarine target.

The conditions under which the groundcrew worked never failed to amaze us. High winds, snow, rain and freezing cold; it was all the same to them. You could return with an unserviceable engine and before you started unloading the aircraft the cowlings would be off and they would be working on the glowing red hot engine with frozen hands. Even overseas, they had to operate in unfriendly conditions, and they would travel with us in the aircraft when we went on detachment. No.269 Squadron was always proud of the close relationship that existed between the two groups of personnel. Even in Ireland it was cold in November and the passage of warm fronts would provide only relative and temporary relief. The flying rations were collected by the Duty NCO and taken to the aircraft. It could be quite a load as they had to provide meals for ten men

over a period that covered three main meals. The only facilities on board were one hot plate with a hot cupboard above it and a hot water urn. Most crews took pride in making each main meal a three course meal. It was amazing what could be achievedunder the dim aircraft lighting; creamed rice looked so much like scrambled eggs when served on toast to the navigator under his yellow lighting!

On arrival at the Squadron the crew would change into flying gear. On cold sorties most would wear a pair of flannel pyjamas under their uniform and then a thick pullover, flying suit and cold weather flying jacket. A few still had the old issue sheepskin lined boots that were not only very warm but extremely comfortable too. All safety equipment and the crew box, containing crockery, cooking utensils and cutlery, would then be transferred to the aircraft and preflight checks would be carried out. Pilots and the engineer would carry out the external aircraft and engine checks while the navigators checked the weapons bay against

their load sheet, to make sure that what they hoped they were going to drop was what they actually dropped. Signallers would stow their gear in the aircraft as their checks could only be carried out with the engines running, the power from the trolley accumulator being too weak to drive both radio and radar. If time permitted, the crew would gather some distance off to have a smoke and savour the silence before engine start. The bulk of the aircraft would loom silhouetted against the lights of the station living quarters on the hill. It was a very reassuring sight. Our usual aircraft was VP287, a Shackleton MR.Mk.1. The Shackleton was the last of the Roy Chadwick designed piston "heavies" and nobody could ask for a better combination than an Avro airframe with Rolls-Royce engines. The overall dependability and surfeit of power did a lot for the peace of mind. When it was time to go, the aircraft was entered through the door on the starboard side. Turning right to go forward, you turned your back on the Elsan toilet and passed the two beam lookout

WR972 retained the Shackleton Mk.3's radar dustbin position, but the radar equipment and housing were not fitted. Instead, a blanking plate was fitted over the radar housing position, incorporating a door. This enabled the position to be used as a parachute door, and various loads were released from this position in support of RAF transport projects. Towards the end of its time with the RAE the aircraft was repainted in a grey, white and blue finish with black engines and black panels across the wings. It was withdrawn in January 1973 when its fatigue life was reached and it was abandoned on Farnborough's fire dump. *(Photos: Paul Platt & Aeroplane)*

positions, the large stores of flares, sea markers and cameras. The next area was designated as the crew rest area but the two rest bunks were always full of parachute bags and more flares, as this is where the illuminating flare guns were mounted. The four banks of six barrels fired one and three quarter million candlepower flares, all at one-second intervals. The resulting string of pearls would light up anything within three quarters of a mile. Just ahead in the fuselage was the galley and the first of the obstacles, the flap activating housing with a cover that was roughly one foot square. Then it was time to climb over one of the main spars past the radar station and over the big main spar which was some three feet wide and high,

passing the navigator and sonics positions on the left side of the fuselage before passing between the engineer's position and the radio position, both of these being small forward facing areas behind the pilots. The two pilot's positions were next and, ducking into the nose, you arrived at the nose canopy with its bench seat for the bomb aimer and observer.

When all stations were manned, the four Rolls-Royce Griffon 57A V-12 engines, each producing 2,455hp would be started in the order of starboard inner, starboard outer, port inner, and port outer. This order ensured that any engine fires could be reached by the ground crew without the problem of turning propellors. With their starting, the constant

roar that would stay with us for fifteen hours commenced. Once all generators were on line and stabilised, the remaining equipment checks could be carried out. The radar scanner was in a chin blister on the nose that allowed performance checks against the hills of Eire across Lough Foyle. Its position would also allow reverse GCAs onto the runways which showed up particularly well when wet - a distinct advantage at Ballykelly. Radio contact would be made on HF with Group control in Scotland and the sonics operators would check the performance of the SARAH Homing equipment against a test set mounted in the control tower. While this took place the navigators checked their GEE, LORAN and the recently fitted Decca

WG530 from No.205 Squadron is pictured in Borneo during 1956. Based at Changi, the unit operated detachments at various sites in the region including Labuan, from where this aircraft was operating at the time this photograph was taken. In common with some other Shackletons operated in the Middle east and Far East, the wing upper surfaces have been painted white as a heat reflection measure. The wing walkway markings (notmally applied in yellow) were switched to red on the white portions of the wings. *(Photo: RAF Air Historical Branch)*

navigator which we would be using on the Squadron's detachment to Christmas Island during the following June. The pilots ran up the engines and checked for magneto drops. Because Ballykelly sits on an old sea floor and is surrounded by hills, everyone in a five-mile radius was more than aware of the condition of the engines, as the sound echoed around the countryside.

The preferred runway at Ballykelly was 26 and this was much more preferable than 20. On runway 20, the old seashore starts where the runway ends and the climb out gradient of the Shackleton then matched the profile of the hills. Taxying a Shackleton Mk.1 in fresh winds was a test of skill and strength. There was no servo assistance to any control

surfaces and the tail wheel was designed to castor, so steering was accomplished by differential braking and variations of engine power. After take-off clearance was obtained, we lined up, checked full and free movement of the controls and after selecting water methanol, applied power against the brakes. Griffons at full song sound sweet and very impressive and when the brakes were released the long take-off run would commence. Once airborne, most vibrations ceased and the engine noise subsided to a mere roar. The prototype Shackleton had soundproofing which was removed from the production models, but no soundproofing could ever help the pilots who sat exactly in line with the eight contra-rotating propellors.

The after take-off checks were followed by the engineer conducting a quick fumes check, after which all equipment could be switched on and normal routine commenced.

Radar was manned continuously by signallers, rotating through the position every 45 minutes to ensure operator efficiency. Crossing coast checks entailed opening the bomb bay and running through weapon selection on the load distributor, and if nothing fell off it was working correctly. Gunnery checks could not be carried out after the removal of the mid upper gun position earlier in the year. Qualified gunners would have to wait until the squadron re-equipped with the Mk.2 with their nose mounted twin 20mm cannon, to resume

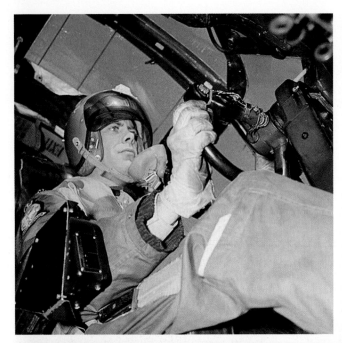

This selection of photographs was taken for RAF publicity purposes shortly after the Shackleton MR.Mk.3 entered service. It shows a typical Shackleton crew at work, with a Signaller capturing photographs from an open beam window, and an Air Gunner inside the forward position ahead of the pilot, who is seen at the controls. Conditions inside the Shackleton were adequate for RAF crews but hardly ideal for the long missions performed by the maritime squadrons. The heating, ventilation, rest and refreshment facilities were gradually improved but the overbearing noise from the Griffon engines was never reduced to more tolerable levels. *(Photos: Aeroplane collection)*

proficiency on the weapon. The mid upper position was a nice sunbathing spot but would occasionally cause an early return to base if the gun blast removed the HF aerials, causing a subsequent loss of communication, should the trailing aerial be ineffectual. It would usually be dark as we tracked north of the Eire coast and set course over Inistrahull Lighthouse. The light of the lighthouse seen from above is a revelation as four or five beams are seen rotating like the spokes on a wheel with the angles between them determining the time intervals of the light flashes. Towards the rear of the aircraft the galley would start operating on a rotating basis of relief every two hours. Coffee was served as soon as possible and after that, silence would descend on the intercom as the crew occupied themselves with their specialist tasks. The three petrol heaters would be fired up (an expression that sometimes all too literally described the

process) and pockets of warmth were established in various parts of the aircraft.

The radio operator maintained contact with Group using a Marconi TR1154/1155 set. It was equipmentthat was designed in the 1940s for ease of use with minimum training, with colour coded controls that linked frequencies and functions. Although low

powered, it had a distinctive chirp that penetrated most static and quite long ranges could be achieved. One of the navigators would act as the en-route navigator while the other would assume the role of tactical navigator if necessary. They would be assisted in their navigation by the radio operator with HF/DF and CONSOL fixes. Drift was measured through a vertical drift sight or by the periscope mounted in the beam area below the aircraft, the latter being used mainly at night with flame floats. Navigation exercises became very boring for those of the crew without jobs and many crews took this opportunity to change positions for training in becoming proficient in other areas. Dawn would reveal the usual grey Atlantic with many whitecaps and large green patches where the sun shone through the clouds on to the sea. The normal cloud cover would dictate a cruising altitude around 800ft, visibility could be unlimited with the absence of haze or smog. Radar would pick up Rockall at 25 miles and a radar practice homing would take place with the operator calling the overhead position with "on top… now, now, now…" commentary. There was always rivalry for proficiency and accuracy, errors of even 25 yards resulting in back chat among the crew. Rockall was the turning point for the southbound leg that crossed the major shipping lanes of the North West Approaches and normally resulted in many sightings to relieve the monotony. Sightings could be infrequent and sometimes when they came there would be two or three. During the last month for instance, we picked up two contacts slightly right of track at 18 and 26 miles. The ASV13's track marker eased the problems experienced with the old Mk.VII, which only had a heading marker. This resulted in the need for a complicated procedure of allowing the target to drift off port or starboard and measuring the angular difference half way to the target and then correcting by doubling the angle and turning the other way. The radar operator called out the range every five miles until the closest target was reported as ten miles. The nose position reported sighting a large passenger liner slightly starboard and on the horizon. The tactical navigator was running a plot and it was decided that this was the further of the two contacts. The closest of the two contacts disappeared at seven miles and the run on that target was finished on directions from the tactical plot. Nothing was seen, and with such a sea running, it would have to have been something large to have provided such a return at that range. We did drop a sonobuoy on the last known position and it was monitored as we headed for the liner. We took the opportunity to increase our stock of ship photographs with a few low passes on both sides. We noted that there was nobody on deck, and we couldn't blame them in that kind of weather. The sonobuoy gave us a bearing on the liner but nothing else. The first contact went down as a disappearing radar contact and was reported as such.

WL801 ended its operational life as an MR.Mk.2 in May 1970, following the disbandment of the ASWDU at St. Mawgan. The aircraft was flown to Kemble and placed in open storage with No.5 Maintenance Unit. Following the decision to operate the Shackleton in the AEW role, WL801 was withdrawn from storage and restored to flying condition, joining No.8 squadron at Lossiemouth on 15 August 1974. This aircraft was not modified to the AEW configuration but retained its MR.Mk.2 equipment, acting as a crew trainer for the squadron. It remained active until its fatigue life expired, at which stage it was ferried to Cosford (11 June 1979) to join No.2 School of Technical Training. It was subsequently declared surplus and dismantled on site. *(Photo: Ashley Annis)*

Radar homings were carried out on most sightings. Most of them would be of freighters and small liners, larger liners like the two Queen Elizabeth ships and the United States being seen further south in the South West Approaches. Lunch would be prepared during these activities and low level manoeuvring during photo runs providing interesting exercises in balancing and dexterity while eating. The meals could consist of four courses, chicken soup followed by steak and kidney pie with potatoes, peas and carrots; finishing with mandarin oranges and cream and coffee - all from cans! The habitability of the interior of the aircraft could have been better of course. The matt black finish and dim lighting became depressing after just a few hours, but after fifteen… Resting members of the crew found it hard to relax, and soundproofing and other amenities would have improved rest and ultimately efficiency, but improvements never came. Six hours after take-off the engines required exercising of the propellor translation units. Each engine would be run through the range of boost and the propellors through the range of RPMs. This provided a welcome variation to the normal synchronised roar. Prior to depth charge drops, we would climb to 3,000ft to check that the area was clear. At the promulgated time the position would be marked with a sea marker that would burn for two hours and the charges would be dropped singly. Everyone would want to see the results of the drop, as it was an annual highlight. The drop would be made by the bomb aimer on a sea marker and a spare crew member would check the weapon's release by observing the bomb bay through a panel in the front bulkhead. Normally, the aircraft would be kept on a steady course to allow observer reports on attack results but in this case everyone wanted to see the effects of the explosion so, after release, a quick turn allowed all a good view of the results. There was a brief time interval after the weapon entered the sea, then a circle of white water flattened the sea with a shock wave, a tall spout reached up 60ft before falling slowly and

causing only a momentary halt to the progress of the Atlantic swells. All this happened in silence as far as we were concerned and, strangely, would have the appearance of slow motion. The remaining three weapons would be dropped and the sortie continued. It looked spectacular but in reality, the weapons had to be within 19ft of the target to be effective. Any attack on a submerging target had to be made within 30 seconds of it disappearing. Nine hours would have passed by this time and course would be set for home. Although the leg was four hours we would complete the detail with two hours on our local radar buoy conducting bombing practice. The intercom would again fall silent as routine was resumed.

The cabin heaters required constant attention and if there was one that would stay on all the time and be super efficient, it was always the one in the navigators' area, bringing complaints of it being too hot. The only crew members occupied were those involved in en-route tasks and off-duty members passed the time as well as they could. The galley supplied coffee and sandwiches and for additional variation, the odd sheet of cardboard was sometimes added to the sandwich filling to see the reaction of those that were busy. Others off duty found their thoughts wandering as they passed the long hours. Books or other reading materials were rarely carried and as many sightings were made in transit, a

lookout was always maintained. The crew was a strange entity. New members served an apprenticeship before being accepted as capable by the rest. The simple reason being that each crew member had the ability to drag all the others along in his own destruction. Although coming from all walks of life they formed a close-knit group, being inseparable and looking after each other, in particular, the new boys in the crew. Of course there were personality tensions and problems but they were always sorted out before becoming too big. In parts of the aircraft the cold permeated flying clothing and members moved around the aircraft to seek warm areas and find company in talking to others. This never happened on fully

Shackleton MR.Mk.1 VP293 was operated in the maritime reconnaissance and anti–submarine warfare role until August 1956 when it was converted to T.Mk.4 trainer standard and delivered to the MOTU at Kinloss in March 1960. It was withdrawn in February 1963 and placed in storage before being transferred to the Royal Aircraft Establishment on 6 January 1964. It was subsequentlt based at Farnborough and assigned to a wide variety of research roles until 23 May 1975 when it reached the end of its fatigue life. It was ferried to the Strathallan collection on 3 May 1976 and remained there for some time. Sadly, the aircraft was allowed to deteriorate (it was kept outdoors) and eventually the airframe was scrapped, with only the nose section being saved for preservation. (Photo: RAE).

operational sorties though, when all positions were manned and everybody had a specific task. We would fly fifteen hours and not see land. The radar operators used these flights to practice different techniques in searching for contacts, switching 'on' and 'off' and searching by sectors in the hope of surprising any submarine that might be using its Electronic Counter Measures equipment to detect our presence. This area was a well-known barren area for submarine operations… but one could always hope.

Radar would pick up the coastline at 45 miles confirming our tracking. The navigators would show no surprise at this (although one or two had missed Ireland in the past). The course would steadily close the coastline

until the loom of Tory Island light was sighted on the horizon. We aimed to pass to the northwest of Tory and set course for Inistrahull and Number Nine radar buoy. The radar buoy was a large moored buoy fitted with radar reflectors designed to match our radar frequencies. Before commencing operations, a safety check would be made of the area and communications established with Ballykelly on VHF. Night bombing was for navigator bomb aiming only and this detail would take more than an hour and a half. Radar homings started at 12-10 miles, the operator gave headings until five miles and then directions left or right until on top. Distances from three miles were called as often as possible, the one mile call including

the phrase "Flares, flares" to start the illuminants. The bomb aimer took over when visual contact was made and the drop made using the bombsight. Assessment of the attack was made by the observer looking rearward through the bomb bay and was made in the form of percentages under and over the target for each bomb as they represented the start and finish of a stick of depth charges. A perfect straddle was with 50-50 no line error - the 'line error' being distances left or right. The result was photographed with a rear-facing camera using six photoflashes from an illuminants discharger in the roof in the beam position. After the run it was out to ten miles again. The illuminants would be reloaded on the

A selection of images showing VP293 at various stages during its time with the Royal Aircraft Establishment. As illustrated, the aircraft arrived at Farnborough in standard RAF maritime colours, complete with red serials (outlined in white under the wings). It then received fluorescent orange markings on its tail, nose wing tips and upper wing leading edges. Standard glossy orange was eventually applied in place of the fluorescent paint and it remained in these markings until it completed its last flight at Farnborough (as illustrated), followed by its final flight to Strathallan airfield (as illustrated).
(Photos: RAE & Tim McLelland collection)

way and a turn would be made back towards the buoy for a repeat performance. Sixteen sticks of practice bombs could require 480 of the l.75 inch projectiles to he loaded and unloaded. The proposed flare activity would have been notified to the Coastguard and Lighthouse services earlier in the day. From the buoy it was only fifteen minutes transit to base and the lights of Derry could be seen reflected off the cloud base over Donegal. It all seemed so close, but the flight had to be fifteen hours long so more flying was needed. On most nights, those not flying were able to relax while sitting in the messes, watching the pretty lights of the flare displays to the northwest. After two hours of bombing, the transit to the circuit was made. Equipment and stores would be packed, washing up done and the aircraft generally tidied prior to landing. The crew brightened up as there would be no need for debriefing after a training exercise and it would be straight to the messes on return. Early morning shaves would have long disappeared and everybody would be conscious of the fact that they had been wearing heavy clothing for almost 18 hours. There would sometimes be debate on

whether the crew would be required to repeat the sortie the next afternoon as was the normal practice when flying hours were the main object of operations. Crossing coast checks included a visual inspection of the bomb bay with the Aldis light to confirm that there were no loose weapons or hang-ups. Tracking in via Magilligan Point and sliding across the northwest face of Benenevagh, the field could be clearly seen on the banks of the Foyle. Benenevagh stands guard at the mouth of the Lough and was known locally as "Ben Twitch". Between Ballykelly and the mountain, the old airfield of Limavady is close to the hill. To warn crews of its closeness, a low powered radio transmitter was used. If the aircraft strayed close to the slopes, the transmitter activated the abandon aircraft klaxons. The circuit was such that it was on and off all the time - hence the "Twitch". Arrival was never a simple process, with the three squadrons and other units, there was always circuit traffic. There was also a further complication in that circuit lengths were sometimes affected by trains crossing the main runway before our arrival, and they always had priority!

After landing, a quick magneto check would be carried out before taxying to dispersal and parking under groundcrew directions. Numbers 1,2 and 4 engines would be cut, number 3 being used to provide services power to open bomb doors and lower flaps to rest the hydraulic system. When number 3 was cut an incredible silence would descend on the aircraft although you could still 'feel' the noise. The opening of the rear door brought a gust of fresh air that accentuated the Shackleton's distinctive smell - that strange mixture of oxygen, leather, sweat, Tepol, hydraulic fluid, paint and electrics - and the Elsan. Outside, the fresh westerly wind felt marvellous and everyone would soon be changed and into cars for the quick run to the mess. Driving off, one would experience the most notable and major effect of a fifteen-hour sortie in a Shackleton - the sound of the oldest Morris Ten car sounding just as good as any Rolls-Royce! ❖

More information and stories on the Shackleton can be found on John's web site at www.avroshackleton.com

114